Mini Skein Knits

25

Knitting Patterns Using
Small Skeins and Leftovers

LARK
New York

LARK
New York

An Imprint of Sterling Publishing
1166 Avenue of the Americas
New York, NY 10036

LARK CRAFTS and the distinctive Lark logo are registered trademarks of Sterling Publishing Co., Inc.

Text © 2015 by Lark Crafts
Photos and Illustrations © 2015 by Lark Crafts
Photography by Rana Faure
Art Direction and Design by Merideth Harte
Illustrations by Orrin Lundgren

ISBN 978-1-4547-0916-9

Distributed in Canada by Sterling Publishing
c/o Canadian Manda Group, 165 Dufferin Street
Toronto, Ontario, Canada M6K 3H6
Distributed in the United Kingdom by GMC Distribution Services
Castle Place, 166 High Street, Lewes, East Sussex, England BN7 1XU
Distributed in Australia by Capricorn Link (Australia) Pty. Ltd.
P.O. Box 704, Windsor, NSW 2756, Australia

For information about custom editions, special sales, and premium and corporate purchases, please contact
Sterling Special Sales at 800-805-5489 or specialsales@sterlingpublishing.com.

Manufactured in China

2 4 6 8 10 9 7 5 3 1

larkcrafts.com

Contents

Introduction

It's hard to resist a mini skein. With their tiny twists and dainty size, they're addictively collectible and the perfect way to play with a wide variety of color. Whether you're buying your mini skeins, participating in a mini skein club or swap, or have that basketful of odds and ends you've been saving, this pattern collection is a must-have.

If you're like me, you may find that mini skeins are easy to collect, but a little tricky to pair with a pattern. The possibilities are endless, but where do you begin? The twenty-five patterns in this book offer something for everyone, from classic stripes to simple stranded knitting to bold colorwork designs. The Basic Techniques section is a great place for the beginner knitter to start or for the more seasoned knitter to refer back to.

Looking for popcorn knitting? The Infinite Rainbow Scarf (page 49) is the perfect choice for mindless stockinette in the round. Looking to try out your first colorwork project? The Head in the Clouds Hat (page 27) uses simple scallops to make a winter wardrobe essential.

A Mermaid Darkly (page 99) is a moody twist on the classic Breton sweater, while the Rainbow Cardi (page 93) is as much fun as a brand-new box of crayons. Both show you that mini skeins aren't just for small-scale projects. Pair a wide variety of colors together for garment knitting.

Chevron accessories make for great statement pieces and you have a choice of striped colorwork with the Lombard Street Scarf (page 57) or simple stranded work with Chevron Boot Toppers (page 67).

Mini skein gradient kits are becoming more and more popular and the Rainy Day Shawl (page 45) is the perfect pattern to let gorgeous gradient take center stage with classic stockinette. For a little colorwork, the Fair Isle Ombre Headband (page 37) shows you how to get creative with a gradient.

Using cotton mini skeins or your cotton odds and ends, you can whip up quick home accessories like the Welcome Spring Oven Towel (page 107) or the Waffle Coasters (page 111).

So gather up those minis and let's get started!

Basic Techniques

We've gathered all the basic techniques you'll need to complete the projects in this book in one place. For the seasoned knitter, this can serve as a refresher course, if needed. For a list of knitting abbreviations, see page 122.

SLIPKNOT

Slipknots are used in knitting and crochet to cast on the first stitch of a project. Start by leaving a tail, then make a loop with the yarn that looks like a cursive *e* (**figure 1**). Holding the area where the yarn crosses with one hand, push a new loop through the existing loop with your other hand (**figure 2**). Place the new loop on the needle or hook and tighten both yarn ends to create the slipknot (**figure 3**).

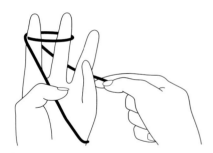

figure 1

figure 2

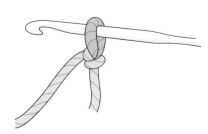

figure 3

KNIT STITCH

For the knit stitch, hold the needle with stitches on it in your left hand, and hold the working yarn in your right hand and at the back of the work. Insert the right-hand needle, from bottom to top, into the stitch as shown (**figure 4**). The tips of the needles will form an *x*. Use your right index finger to wrap the strand of yarn, counterclockwise, around the right-hand needle (**figure 5**). Bring the yarn through the stitch with the right-hand needle and pull the loop off the left-hand needle (**figure 6**). You now have one complete knit stitch on your right-hand needle. Continue until the end of the row, or as the pattern directs.

figure 4

figure 5

figure 6

PURL STITCH

For the purl stitch, hold the needle with the stitches on it in your left hand. Hold the working yarn in your right hand and at the front of your work. Insert the right-hand needle, from top to bottom, into the stitch (**figure 7**). Using your right index finger, wrap the strand of yarn counterclockwise around the right-hand needle (**figure 8**). Bring the yarn through the stitch with the right-hand needle and pull the loop off the left-hand needle (**figure 9**). Continue until the end of the row, or as the pattern directs.

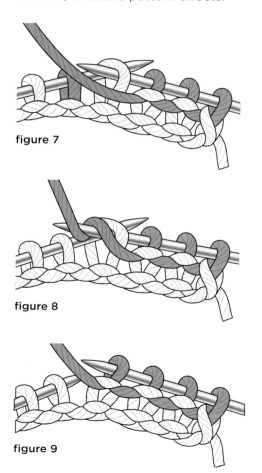

figure 7

figure 8

figure 9

YARN OVER (YO)

Bring the working yarn to the front and knit the stitch normally. This wraps the yarn around the needle, creating a yarn over (**figure 10**).

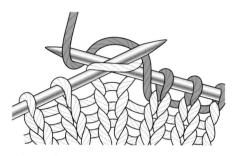

figure 10

SLIP STITCH PURLWISE

Slipping a stitch means you pass a stitch from one needle to another without working it. A slip stitch purlwise won't twist, as it does knitwise. To slip one stitch purlwise, insert your right needle into the next stitch on your left needle as though purling the stitch. Pull the stitch off your left needle; the stitch will now be on the right needle (**figure 11**).

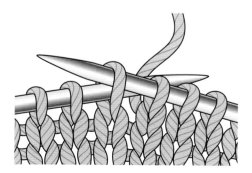

figure 11

PICKING UP STITCHES

To pick up stitches along a bound-off edge, insert your needle into the space under both loops of the existing stitch (**figure 12**). Bring the yarn under the needle and scoop it through the hole to create one stitch on the needle. *Insert the needle into the next space, wrap the yarn counterclockwise, and scoop the loop through the space. Repeat from * until you've picked up the desired number of stitches (**figure 13**).

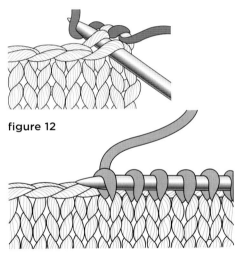

figure 12

figure 13

CAST-ONS
Longtail Cast-on

Calculate about 1 inch/2.5cm of yarn per stitch that you'll be casting on; this will be your tail. Letting the tail hang, tie a slipknot around one of your knitting needles. You'll now have two strands of yarn hanging down from your needle—the tail and the strand connected to the ball (**figure 14**). Placing the needle in your right hand, separate the two strands of yarn

with your left thumb and index finger. Secure both loose ends under your ring finger and pinky (**figure 15**). Use your needle to scoop under the outer strand of the thumb loop (**figure 16**) then over the inner strand of the index finger loop (**figure 17**). Let the loop fall off your thumb (**figure 18**) and pull the tail so the stitch fits loosely onto your needle. Repeat until you've cast on the desired number of stitches.

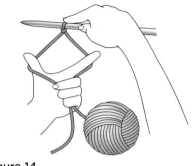

figure 14

figure 15

figure 16

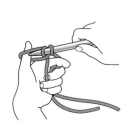

figure 17

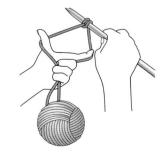

figure 18

Provisional Cast-on

Using a needle at least one size larger than what your pattern calls for and a length of waste yarn at least 3 times longer than the length of your finished cast-on, make a slipknot with the working yarn and place it on the needle. Hold the needle and one end of the waste yarn in your right hand (**figure 19**). *Move the working yarn in front and under the waste yarn (**figure 20**) and then in front and over the needle (**figure 21**).* Repeat from * to * until you have the correct number of loops of working yarn on the needle. Finish by moving the working yarn in front and under the waste yarn (**figure 22**).

Cable Cast-on

Start with a slipknot on the left-hand needle. Keep the tail on the left and the working yarn on your right (**figure 23**). Knit into the slipknot with your right-hand needle (**figure 24**). Slip the new stitch you just made from your right-hand needle to your left-hand needle (**figure 25**). *Knit into the stitch you slipped to your left-hand needle (**figure 26**). Slip the new stitch you just made from your right-hand needle to your left-hand needle (**figure 27**).* Repeat from * to * until you have the number of cast-on stitches necessary.

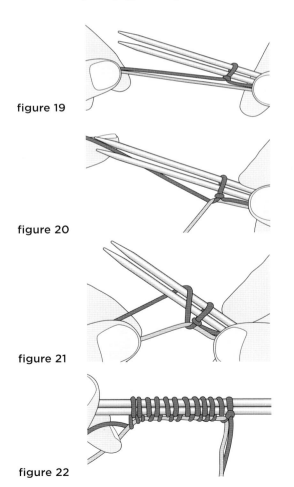

figure 19

figure 20

figure 21

figure 22

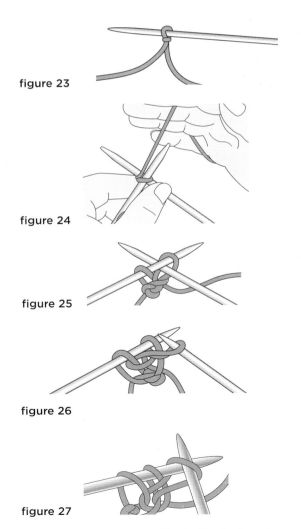

figure 23

figure 24

figure 25

figure 26

figure 27

BIND-OFFS
Basic Knit Bind-Off

Knit two stitches. *With the tip of your left-hand needle, pull the second stitch on the right-hand needle over the first (**figure 28**) and let it drop off. You'll now have one stitch left on the needle (**figure 29**). Knit another stitch and repeat from * (**figure 30**). Continue in this manner, or as the pattern directs, until you have one stitch remaining on your left-hand needle. Break yarn and pull the tail through the last stitch to fasten off.

figure 28

figure 29

figure 30

Sewn Bind-Off

Break off a length of yarn about three times as long as the knitting, and thread it onto a yarn needle. *Insert the needle into the first two stitches on the knitting needle as if to purl and draw the yarn through (**figure 31**). Reinsert the needle into the first stitch on the knitting needle as if to knit, draw yarn through, then slip the stitch off (**figure 32**).* Repeat from * to *.

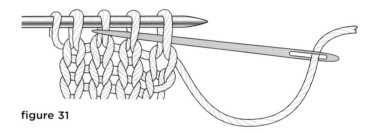

figure 31

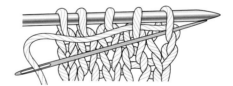

figure 32

Three-Needle Bind-Off

*With the wrong side of each knitted piece facing out, and the needles parallel (**figure 33**), slip a third (working) needle into the first stitch of both needles simultaneously (**figure 34**). Wrap the yarn around the working needle as if to knit, and pull a loop through (**figure 35**). Allow the first stitch from each of the parallel needles to fall from the needles (**figure 36**).* Repeat from * to * until you have one stitch remaining on each working needle. Using one of the two parallel needles, pass the first stitch on the working needle over the second stitch and off the needle as you normally would when binding off (**figure 37**). Break yarn and pull the tail through the last stitch to fasten off.

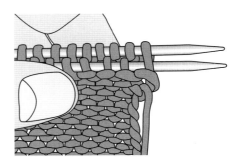

figure 33

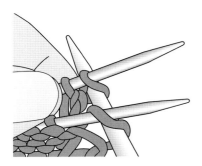

figure 34

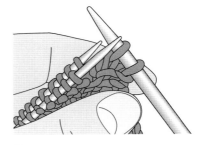

figure 35

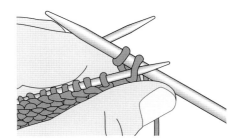

figure 36

figure 37

Kitchener Stitch

The Kitchener stitch is a technique to invisibly weave together live stitches. Thread a tapestry needle with the same yarn you used to work your project (preferably the tail of your working yarn). Hold the needles with the live stitches parallel in your left hand (**figure 38**). Insert the tapestry needle through the first stitch on the front needle as if to purl, pull the yarn through, leaving a tail that you will weave in later (**figure 39**). Leave the stitch on the front needle. Insert the tapestry needle through the first stitch on the back needle as if to knit, pull the yarn through, leaving the stitch on the back needle (**figure 40**). *Insert the tapestry needle through the first stitch on the front needle as if to knit, pull the yarn through, removing the stitch

from the front needle (**figure 41**). Insert the tapestry needle through the next stitch on the front needle as if to purl, pull the yarn through, leaving the stitch on the front needle (**figure 42**). Insert the tapestry needle through the first stitch on the back needle as if to purl, pull the yarn through, removing the stitch on the back needle (**figure 43**). Insert the tapestry needle through the next stitch on the back needle as if to knit, pull the yarn through, leaving the stitch on the back needle (**figure 44**).* Repeat from * to * until all stitches have been worked. Every few stitches, adjust the tension of your work, making sure not to pull too tightly. Remember, you are making an extra row of knitting, rather than sewing together a seam.

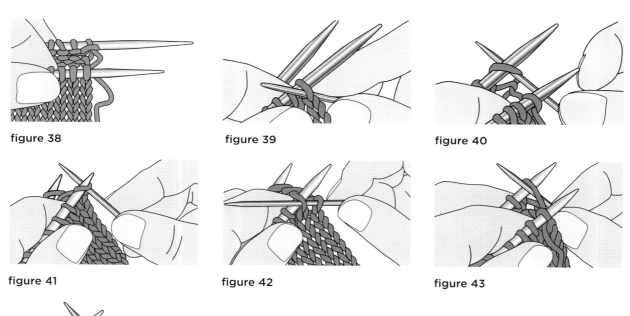

figure 38

figure 39

figure 40

figure 41

figure 42

figure 43

figure 44

INCREASES
Make One Left (m1L)

Insert left-hand needle from the front to the back under the horizontal strand between the stitch just worked and the next stitch (**figure 45**), knit the lifted strand through the back loop (**figure 46**).

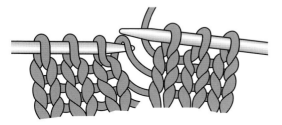

figure 45

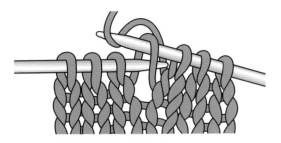

figure 46

Make One Right (m1R)

Insert left-hand needle from back to front under the horizontal strand between the stitch just worked and the next stitch (**figure 47**), knit the lifted strand through the front loop (**figure 48**).

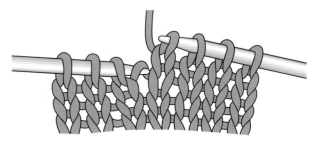

figure 47

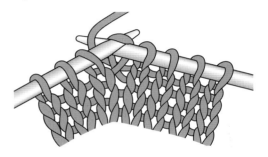

figure 48

Knit Front and Back (kfb)

Knit the next stitch but do not remove the stitch from the left knitting needle (**figure 49**). Insert the right-hand knitting needle behind the left-hand knitting needle and knit again into the back of the same stitch (**figure 50**). Slip the original stitch off the left-hand knitting needle.

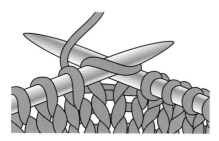

figure 49

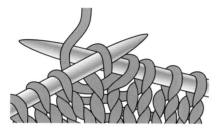

figure 50

Purl Front and Back (pfb)

Purl the next stitch but do not remove the stitch from the left-hand knitting needle (**figure 51**). Insert the right-hand knitting needle behind the left-hand knitting needle and purl again into the back of the same stitch (**figure 52**). Slip the original stitch off the left-hand knitting needle.

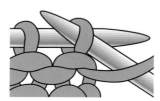

figure 51

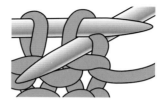

figure 52

Purl Two Together (p2tog)

Insert needle into the next two stitches on the left-hand needle as if to purl. Purl both stitches together as if they were one (**figure 54**).

figure 54

Slip, Slip, Knit (ssk)

Slip your next two stitches, one at a time, onto the right-hand needle (**figure 55**). Insert the tip of the left-hand needle into the fronts of these stitches (**figure 56**), from left to right, and knit them together.

figure 55

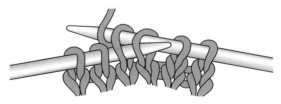

figure 56

DECREASES
Knit Two Together (k2tog)

Insert needle into the next two stitches on the left-hand needle as if to knit. Knit both stitches together as if they were one (**figure 53**).

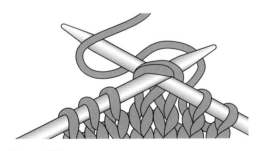

figure 53

Sl1-k2tog-psso

Slip one stitch knitwise (**figure 57**), knit two stitches together (**figure 58**), pass the slipped stitch over (**figure 59**) (two stitches decreased).

figure 57

figure 58

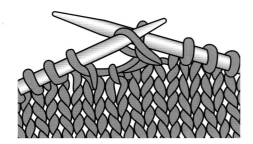

figure 59

WRAP AND TURN (W+T)
Wrap on the Knit Side

Keep the working yarn in back and slip the next stitch on the left-hand needle onto the right-hand needle, purlwise (**figure 60**). Bring the yarn to the back between the needles and slip the stitch from the right-hand needle back to the left-hand needle (**figure 61**). Turn your work. The yarn is now correctly positioned to purl.

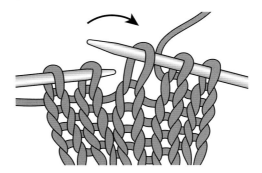

figure 60

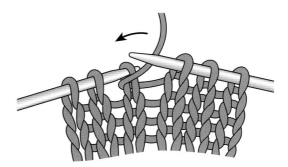

figure 61

Pick Up Wrapped Stitches on the Knit Side

Pick up the wrap with the right-hand needle from front to back (**figure 62**). Then insert the right-hand needle into the stitch that is wrapped (**figure 63**). Knit the wrap and the stitch together (**figure 64**).

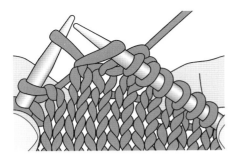

figure 62

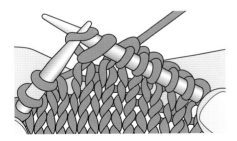

figure 63

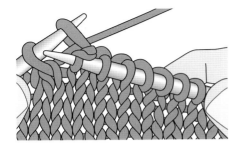

figure 64

Wrap on the Purl Side

Keep the yarn in front. Slip the next stitch on the left-hand needle onto the right-hand needle, purlwise (**figure 65**). Bring the yarn to the back between the needles (**figure 66**). Then slip the stitch from the right-hand needle back to the left (**figure 67**). Turn your work. Bring the yarn to the back between the needles to knit.

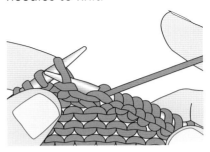

figure 65

figure 66

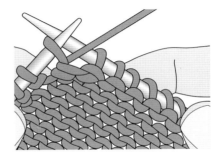

figure 67

Picking Up the Wrapped Stitch on the Purl Side

Pick up the wrap with the right-hand needle from back to front (**figure 68**). Place the wrap onto the left-hand needle (**figure 69**). Purl together the wrap and the stitch that is wrapped (**figure 70**).

Weave in Ends

Insert tail of working yarn into a tapestry needle and weave the loose ends of yarn in and out of the stitches on the wrong side of the work. Whenever possible, weave the ends into seam lines (**figure 71**).

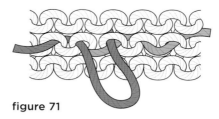

figure 71

figure 68

figure 69

figure 70

For the Head, Neck & Shoulders

Head in the Clouds Hat

This slightly slouchy beanie with soft scallops will become your new go-to hat. Knitting fingering-weight yarn with larger needles provides excellent drape for a casual look.

SKILL LEVEL: Easy

Finished Measurements:
One size, approx 20–22″/51–56cm in circumference (will stretch to fit a range of sizes)

Materials and Tools
> Madelinetosh Unicorn Tails (100% superwash merino wool; 1 skein per color, or approx 52yds/48m of fingering-weight yarn per color): (A), onyx; (B), dirty panther; (C), dust bowl; (D), antique lace; (E), antler.
> Size 3 US (3.25mm) double-pointed needles or 40″/101.5cm circular needle (for magic loop)
> Size 5 US (3.75mm) double-pointed needles, or 40″/101.5cm circular needle (for magic loop), or size needed to obtain gauge
> Stitch marker
> Tapestry needle

Gauge
> 26 sts/35 rows = 4″/10cm on size 5 US (3.75mm) needles in the round, post-blocking
> *Always take time to check your gauge.*

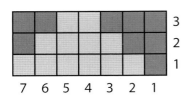

INSTRUCTIONS

With smaller needles, CO 140 sts with color A. Join to knit in the round, placing marker at BOR.
Rnds 1–18: *(K2, p2), rep from *.
Change to larger needles.
Rnds 19–21: Work in stockinette (k every st).
Rnds 22–24: Follow chart for scallop pattern, transitioning to color B.
Rnds 25–37: Work in stockinette in color B. Repeat rnds 22–37 two more times, transitioning through colors C and D.
Next 3 rnds: Follow chart for scallop pattern, transitioning from color D to E.
Next rnds: Knit in stockinette for 10 rnds.

Shape Crown:

Next rnd (dec rnd): *K5, k2tog, rep from * around—120 sts.
Next rnd: *K4, k2tog, rep from * around—100 sts.
Next rnd: *K3, k2tog, rep from * around—80 sts.
Next rnd: *K2, k2tog, rep from * around—60 sts.
Next rnd: *K1, k2tog, rep from * around—40 sts.
Next rnd: K2tog around—20 sts.
Break yarn, leaving a long tail. Using tapestry needle, thread yarn tail through remaining sts and pull to tighten. Weave in ends to secure.

DESIGNED BY *Yelena M. Dasher*

Crazy Color Trio: Hat, Cowl & Mittens

Banish winter with this bright, happy trio that will keep you warm and keep the gray at bay.

SKILL LEVEL: Easy

CRAZY COLOR HAT

Finished Measurements:

17"/43cm in circumference unstretched
(will fit an average adult woman)

Materials and Tools

> A-H: Colour Adventures Cloud in DK (80% superwash merino wool, 10% cashmere, 10% nylon; 230yd/210m per 100g): (A), georgin; (B), marigold; (D), blush; (E), lemon; (F), fresh leaves; (G), blue bell; and (H), forget-me-not; Astral Bath Yarns Spectra in DK (100% superwash merino wool; 250yd/229m per 115g) in (C), rum sodomy and the lash. Eight different colors of any DK weight yarn will work, though I would suggest mostly wool for blends, 25yd/23m per color.

> Two size 5 US (3.75mm) 24"/61cm circular needles (or preferred length for large-circumference knitting in the round)

> Tapestry needle

Gauge

> 22 sts/32 rows = 4"/10cm in stockinette stitch without colorwork

> 25 sts/32 rows = 4"/10cm in stockinette stitch with colorwork

> *Always take time to check your gauge.*

INSTRUCTIONS

With B cast on 108 stitches.

Join to work in the round, pm for BOR.

Rnds 1–12: Work in k1, p1 ribbing.

Rnd 13: Work row 1 of chart.

Continue working from chart as established until all rows of the chart have been completed.

Shape Crown:

Work crown shaping with B.

Next rnd: (K10, k2tog) 9 times—99 sts.

Next rnd: Knit.

Next rnd: (K9, k2tog) 9 times—90 sts.

Next rnd: Knit.

Next rnd: (K8, k2tog) 9 times—81 sts.

Next rnd: Knit.

Next rnd: (K7, k2tog) 9 times—72 sts.

Next rnd: Knit.

Next rnd: (K6, k2tog) 9 times—63 sts.

Next rnd: Knit.

Next rnd: (K5, k2tog) 9 times—54 sts.

Next rnd: Knit.

Next rnd: (K4, k2tog) 9 times—45 sts.

Knit 1 round.

Next rnd: (K3, k2tog) 9 times—36 sts.

Next rnd: (K2, k2tog) 9 times—27 sts.

Next rnd: (K1, k2tog) 9 times—18 sts.

Next rnd: K2tog around—9 sts.

Cut yarn, leaving enough yarn to thread through the remaining 9 stitches and pull tightly to close the hole.

Finishing:

Weave in all ends, making sure to tightly close any stitches that gap due to the color changes.

Crazy Color Hat chart

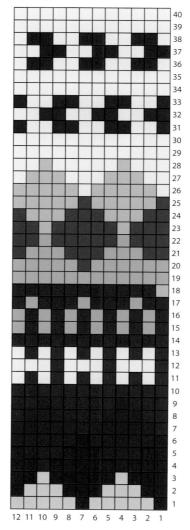

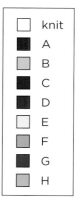

CRAZY COLOR COWL

Finished Measurements:

23"/58.5cm in circumference unstretched (will fit an average adult)

Materials and Tools

> A–I: Colour Adventures Cloud in DK (80% superwash merino wool, 10% cashmere, 10%

nylon; 230yd/210m per 100g): (A), georgin;
(B), marigold; (D), blush; (E), lemon; (F),
fresh leaves; (G), blue bell; and (H), forget-
me-not; Astral Bath Yarns Spectra in DK
(100% superwash merino wool; 250yd/229m
per 115g) in (C), rum sodomy and the lash;
Madelinetosh DK Twist (100% superwash
merino wool; 250yd/229m per 120g) in (I),
tundra; Nine different colors of any DK weight
yarn will work, though I would suggest mostly
wool for blends, 25yd/23m per color.)

> Two size 5 US (3.75mm) 24"/61cm circular
  needles (or preferred length for large-
  circumference knitting in the round)
> Tapestry needle

Gauge

> 22 sts/32 rows = 4"/10cm in stockinette stitch
  without colorwork
> 25 sts/32 rows = 4"/10cm in stockinette stitch
  with colorwork
> *Always take time to check your gauge.*

INSTRUCTIONS

With F, cast on 144 stitches.

Join to work in the round, pm for BOR.

Rnds 1–8: Work in k1, p1 ribbing.

Rnd 9: Work row 1 of chart.

Continue working from chart as established until
all rows of the chart have been completed.

Next rnds: With F, work 8 rounds in k1, p1 ribbing

Finishing:

Bind off all sts.

Weave in all ends, making sure to tightly close
any stitches that gap due to the color changes.

Crazy Color Cowl chart

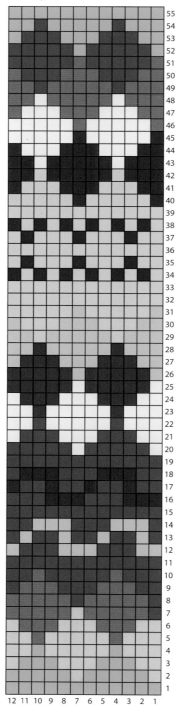

☐	knit
▨	F
▨	B
▨	I
▨	C
▨	H
■	A
☐	E
▨	D
■	G

CRAZY COLOR MITTENS

Finished Measurements:

7"/18cm in circumference at the widest part of the hand, not including thumb, unstretched (will fit an average adult woman's hand)

Materials and Tools

> **A-J**: Colour Adventures Cloud in DK (80% superwash merino wool, 10% cashmere, 10% nylon; 230yd/210m per 100g): (A), georgin; (B), marigold; (D), blush; (E), lemon; (F), fresh leaves; (G), blue bell; (H), forget-me-not; (I), grey; Astral Bath Yarns Spectra in DK (100% superwash merino wool; 250yd/229m per 115g) in (C), rum sodomy and the lash; Madelinetosh DK Twist (100% superwash merino wool; 250yd/229m per 120g) in (J), tundra; Ten different colors of any DK weight yarn will work, though I would suggest mostly wool for blends, 25yd/23m per color.

> Two size 5 US (3.75mm) 24"/61cm circular needles (or preferred length for large-circumference knitting in the round and preferred method for small-circumference knitting in the round, i.e., 16"/40.5cm circular needle, DPNs; instructions in the pattern assume knitting the sleeves on two circular needles)

> Stitch holder or waste yarn

> Tapestry needle

Gauge

> 22 sts/32 rows = 4"/10cm in stockinette stitch without colorwork

> 23 sts/32 rows = 4"/10cm in stockinette stitch with colorwork

> *Always take time to check your gauge.*

INSTRUCTIONS

Mitten (make 2)

With C, cast on 40 stitches.

Join to work in the round, pm for BOR.

Rnds 1–12: Work in k1, p1 ribbing.

Rnd 13: Work row 1 of chart.

Rnds 14–23: Continue working from chart.

Shape Thumb Gusset:

Rnd 24: Work next row of chart until 1 st before EOR, pm, m1R, k1, m1L—42 sts (3 sts following marker).

Rnds 25–26: Work next 2 rows of chart, working all stitches after the marker in the dominant color of the round; changing that color when the dominant color changes.

Rnd 27: Work next row of chart to marker, sm, m1R, k to end, m1L—44 sts (5 sts following marker).

Rnds 28–45: Repeat rnds 25–27 until there are 17 stitches after the marker—56 sts. *Note:* You will have worked through row 33 of the chart.

Next rnd: Work next row of chart to marker, place 17 stitches on waste yarn for thumb, CO 1 st—40 sts.

Continue working chart as established through the end of the chart.

Shape Top of Mitten:

Continuing with C, (k1, ssk, k14, k2tog, k1) 2 times—36 sts.

Knit 2 rnds.

Next rnd: (K1, ssk, k12, k2tog, k1) 2 times—32 sts.

Knit 2 rnds.

Next rnd: (K1, ssk, k10, k2tog, k1) 2 times—28 sts.

Knit 2 rnds.

Next rnd: (K1, ssk, k8, k2tog, k1) 2 times—24 sts.

Knit 2 rnds.

Next rnd: (K1, ssk, k6, k2tog, k1) 2 times—20 sts.

Knit 2 rnds.

Next rnd: (K1, ssk, k4, k2tog, k1) 2 times—16 sts.

Graft remaining 16 stitches using Kitchener stitch.

Thumb:

Place 10 of the thumb stitches on 1 needle and
the other 7 thumb stitches on a 2nd needle.
Pick up and knit 3 stitches from the gap and
join to work in the round, using the color that
corresponds to the dominant color from the
round of the mitten body—20 sts. Match the
color changes to those on the mitten body every
five rounds.

Knit 15 rnds.

Rnd 16: K1, k2tog, k to last 3 sts, ssk, k1—18 sts.

Rnd 17: Knit.

Rnd 18: (K1, k2tog) to end—12 sts.

Rnd 19: K2tog to end—6 sts.

Cut yarn, leaving enough yarn to thread through
the remaining 6 stitches and pull tightly to close
the hole.

Finishing:

Weave in all ends, making sure to tightly close
any stitches that gap due to the color changes.

Crazy Color Mittens chart

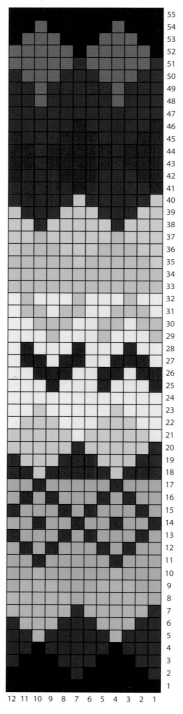

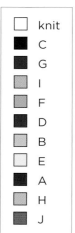

☐	knit
■	C
■	G
■	I
■	F
■	D
■	B
☐	E
■	A
■	H
■	J

DESIGNED BY *Holly Chayes*

Fair Isle Ombre Headband

A simple Fair Isle headband, designed to warm your ears without ruining your hair. Knit in a tube, with the ends grafted shut, five colors of mini skeins combined to create five Fair Isle color combinations for a beautiful ombre effect.

SKILL LEVEL: Intermediate

Finished Measurements:
Relaxed: 3"/7.5cm wide x 20"/51cm long
Stretched: 2½"/6.5cm wide x 24"/61cm long

Materials and Tools
> One set of Julie Asselin Leizu Fingering Gradient Set colorway vendanges (90% superwash merino wool and 10% silk; includes five mini skeins from darkest to lightest in color, 105yd/96m per 1oz skein; 525yd/480m total, fingering-weight yarn)
> Set of DPNs, size 3 US (3.25mm)
> Stitch marker and Tapestry needle

Gauge
> 36 sts/34 rows to 4"/10cm in washed and blocked checkerboard Fair Isle pattern
> *Always take time to check your gauge.*

INSTRUCTIONS:

Arrange colors from darkest to lightest. Darkest color is color A, lightest color is color E.

Using A, CO 60 sts. Join in the round, being careful not to twist. Pm to mark beginning of the round.

Work rnds 1–40 of colorwork chart four times.

Work rnds 1–8 of colorwork chart once.

Using A, BO all stitches.

Finishing:

Weave in all ends. Wash and block.

Using a tapestry needle and leftover yarn of color A, seam CO and BO edges together in a tube.

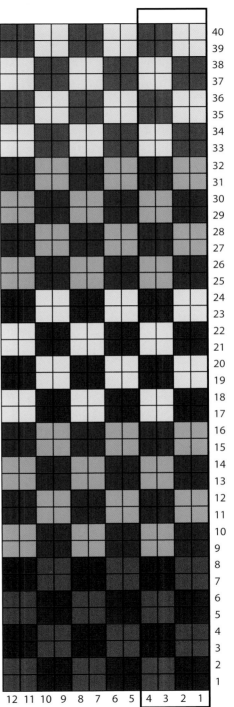

	A
	B
	C
	D
	E

DESIGNED BY *Dana E. Freed*

Line Intersection: Color Study in Blue

Vertical, horizontal, and diagonal bands of color and texture intersect in this large-gradient shawl. Hues of the same color, arranged from dark to light, create a dramatic effect. Simple bias shaping, in combination with stitch striping, create a piece that is both fun to make and easy to wear.

SKILL LEVEL: Intermediate

Finished Measurements:
Approx 88"/224cm x 18"/46cm after blocking

Materials and Tools

> Dragonfly Fibers Traveller Gradient Set (100% superwash merino wool; six 2oz/57g skeins, 140yd/128m each): (A), darkest color; (B); (C); (D); (E); (F), lightest color—840yd/768m total DK weight yarn. Shown in colorway cheshire cat.

> Size 9 US (5.5mm) 32"/81cm or longer circular needle

> Darning or tapestry needle

Gauge

> 17 sts/28 rows = 4"/10cm

> *Always take time to check your gauge.*

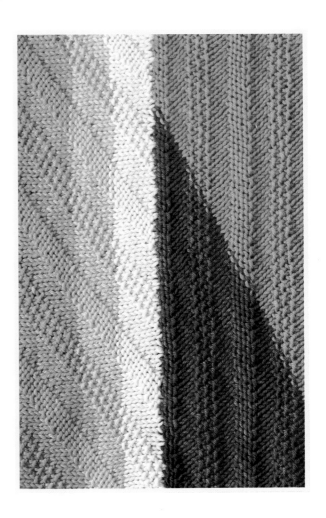

INSTRUCTIONS

With color A, CO 85 sts.

Setup row (RS): *P5, k5, p1, k1, p1, k1, p1, k5; rep from * to last 5 sts, p5.

Row 1 (WS): Kfb, k3, p5, k1, p1, k1, p1, k1, p5; *k5, p5, k1, p1, k1, p1, k1, p5; rep from * to last 6 sts, k4, k2tog.

Row 2 (RS): P2tog, p4, k5, p1, k1, p1, k1, p1, k5; *p5, k5, p1, k1, p1, k1, p1, k5; rep from * to last 4 sts, p3, pfb.

Rows 3–26: Rep rows 1–2 twelve more times.

Row 27: Rep row 1 once more—28 rows total in color A.

Change to color B.
Rep rows 1–2 fourteen times—28 rows total in color B.

Change to color C.
Rep rows 1–2 fourteen times—28 rows total in color C.

Change to color D.
Rep rows 1–2 fourteen times—28 rows total in color D.

Change to color E.
Rep rows 1–2 fourteen times—28 rows total in color E.

Change to color F.
Rep rows 1–2 fourteen times—28 rows total in color F.
BO all sts knitwise.

With RS facing, hold the piece so that color A is on the left and color F is on the right. Using color F, pick up 245 sts across the long side of the work starting at the color F edge and working toward color A.

Row 1 (WS): K2tog, k4, p5, k1, p1, k1, p1, k1, p5; *k5, p5, k1, p1, k1, p1, k1, p5; rep from * to last 4 sts, k3, kfb.

Row 2 (RS): Pfb, p3, k5, p1, k1, p1, k1, p1, k5; *p5, k5, p1, k1, p1, k1, p1, k5; rep from * to last 6 sts, p4, p2tog.

Rep rows 1–2 two more times.
Rep row 1 once more—8 rows total in color F including pickup row.

Change to color E.
Rep rows 1–2 four times—8 rows total in color E.

Change to color D.
Rep rows 1–2 four times—8 rows total in color D.

Change to color C.
Rep rows 1–2 four times—8 rows total in color C.

Change to color B.
Rep rows 1–2 four times—8 rows total in color B.

Change to color A.
Rep rows 1–2 three times.
Rep row 1 once more—7 rows total in color A.
BO all sts knitwise.

Finishing:
Weave in all ends.
Block.

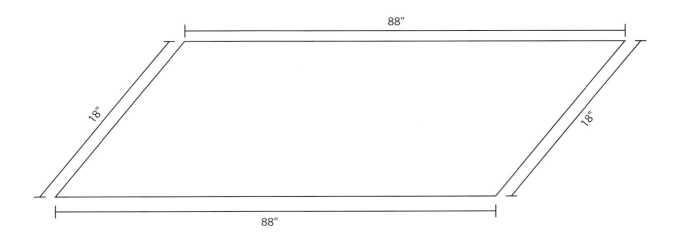

DESIGNED BY *Deborah Stack*

Rainy Day Shawl

Gradient yarns are so much fun to work with. Whether you're working with gently transitioning shades or dramatic and colorful ombres, part of the fun of knitting with these yarns is watching the colors transition before your eyes. This pattern is a simple shawl, ideal for beginners, and places the spotlight on your yarn—perfect for solid gradients, but also well suited for variegation and stripes alike.

SKILL LEVEL: Easy

Finished Measurements:
Approx 25"/63.5cm long x 40"/101.5cm wide across top edge.

Materials and Tools

> 2 packages of Copper Corgi Gradient Mini-Skein Set in colorway clifftop (100% superwash merino wool; 360yd/329m per package, 6 mini skeins per package [60yd/55m per mini skein]) —approx 720yd/658m total in sport weight yarn (*Note:* In this project, mini skeins were alternated to ensure a perfect gradient. First, work with the lightest color from each package, then use the 2nd lightest color from both packages, and so on.)
> Size 6 US (4mm) needles

Gauge:

> 23 sts/30 rows = 4"/10cm in stockinette stitch
> *Always take time to check your gauge.*

INSTRUCTIONS

Provisionally cast on 3 stitches (**figure 1**).

(*Note*: In the pictured shawl, the cast-on is performed with the lightest shade first.)

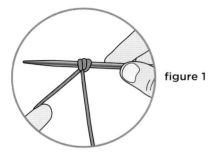

figure 1

Knit 6 rows (**figure 2**).

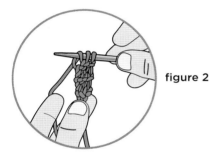

figure 2

Do not turn work. Using working yarn, pick up (**figure 3**) and knit 3 sts down the side of the knit strip (**figure 4**).

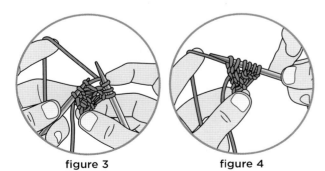

figure 3

figure 4

Undo provisional cast-on and place live sts on the needle. Knit to end of row—9 sts (**figure 5**).

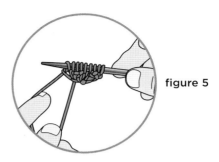

figure 5

Row 1 (WS): K3, pm, p1, pm, p1, pm, p1, pm, k3.

Row 2 (RS): K3, sm, yo, knit to marker, yo, sm, k1, sm, yo, knit to marker, yo, sm, K3—13 sts.

Row 3 (WS): K3, sm, p to last 3 sts (slipping markers as you go), k3.

Repeat rows 2–3 eighty times—333 sts.

Lace Border:

Row 1 (RS): K3, sm, yo, *k2tog, yo, repeat from * to 1 st before marker, k1, yo, sm, k1, sm, yo, k1, yo, **ssk, yo, repeat from ** to next marker, sm, k3—337 sts.

Row 2 (WS): K3, sm, p to last 3sts, slipping markers as you go, k3.

Row 3 (RS): K3, sm, yo, k1, yo, *ssk, yo, repeat from * to next marker, sm, k1, sm, yo, **k2tog, yo, repeat from ** to last 4 sts. K1, yo, sm, k3—341 sts.

Row 4 (WS): K3, sm, p to last 3 sts, slipping markers as you go, k3.

Repeat rows 1–4 of lace border 2 more times—357 sts.

Repeat rows 1–2 once more—361 sts.

Finishing:

Loosely bind off. Weave in ends. Wet-block shawl, taking care to pin out lace border.

DESIGNED BY *Connie Santisteban*

Infinite Rainbow Cowl

Even on a blustery, cold winter day, you can carry a rainbow with you wherever you go.

SKILL LEVEL: Easy

Finished Measurements:

52"/132cm long x 7½"/19cm wide after blocking but before grafting ends together or 26"/66cm long x 7½"/19cm wide after blocking and grafting ends together

Materials and Tools

> Two size 5 US (3.75mm) circular needles with 16"/40.5cm cables
> 2 skeins Madelinetosh Sport (100% superwash merino wool; 270yd/247m or 540yd/494m of sport weight yarn): (MC), gossamer
> Western Sky Knits Rainbow Mini Skein Set Willow Superwash Sport, (100% merino wool, 50yd/46m per color or 50yd/46m of 7 colors of sport weight mini skeins): (A), red; (B), orange; (C), yellow; (D), green; (E), blue; (F), purple; (G) magenta
> Waste yarn
> Stitch marker
> Crochet hook
> Tapestry needle

Gauge

> 26 sts/24 rows = 4"/10cm in stockinette stitch
> *Always take time to check your gauge.*

INSTRUCTIONS

Using MC, provisionally cast on 100 sts. Place stitch marker on needles to mark BOR and join to work in the round.

Rnds 1–7: Knit and do not cut yarn. You will carry up the MC throughout.

Rnds 8–12: Switch to A and k. Cut yarn.

Rnds 13–19: Switch to MC and k.

Rnds 20–24: Switch to B and k. Cut yarn.

Rnds 25–31: Switch to MC and k.

Rnds 32–36: Switch to C and k. Cut yarn.

Rnds 37–43: Switch to MC and k.

Rnds 44–48: Switch to D and k. Cut yarn.

Rnds 49–55: Switch to MC and k.

Rnds 56–60: Switch to E and k. Cut yarn.

Rnds 61–67: Switch to MC and k.

Rnds 68–72: Switch to F and k. Cut yarn.

Rnds 73–79: Switch to MC and k.

Rnds 80–84: Switch to G and k. Cut yarn.

Repeat rnds 1–84 three times (four rainbow repeats), but on rnd 84 of the 4th repeat do not cut G. Slip off the stitch marker.

Using G, measure 4 times the circumference of your work and cut yarn. This will be used to graft your project closed. Keep these stitches on the needle.

Finishing:

Turn the scarf inside out and weave in all ends except the final rnd of G.

Turn the scarf right side out, unpick the provisional CO, and transfer it onto your 2nd circular needle.

Make sure your tube is not twisted and graft the ends together using Kitchener stitch.

DESIGNED BY *Carol J. Sulcoski*

Jewel Box Shawl

This cozy shawl knits up in a flash in handpainted worsted-weight yarn. Easy enough for a beginner, it's also perfect for times when you need to kick back and work on something relaxing. The sample uses eight different mini skeins, but you can adapt the number of stripes to whatever you have on hand, rounding out your mini skeins with leftover balls from other projects.

SKILL LEVEL: Beginner

Finished Measurements:

Length at top edge: approx 40″/127cm
Height at center: approx 17″/47cm

Materials and Tools

> Black Bunny Fibers Workhorse Wool Miniskeins (100% superwash merino wool; 40g = 80yd/73m): 1 mini skein each of (A) tealarific; (B) dusted mauve; (C) raspberry jam; (D) leaf; (E) indigo-go; (F) cerise; (G) cement; and (H) golf course—640yd/585m total of worsted-weight yarn (*Note:* Feel free to use as many or as few mini skeins as you wish, ending the old color on a row 4 and beginning a new color on the transition row, or use additional mini skeins to create a larger shawl.)

> Size 9 US (5.5mm) needles, 32″/81cm or 36″/91cm circular needles or size needed to obtain gauge

> Two stitch markers

> Tapestry needle

Gauge

> 16 sts/24 rows = 4″/10cm in stockinette stitch

> *Always take time to check your gauge.*

INSTRUCTIONS

Note: Shawl is knit from the bottom up, working horizontally. First and last four sts of each row, excluding top and bottom edges, are garter stitch.

With color A, CO 4, pm, CO 88, pm, CO 4 sts—96 sts.

Knit 6 rows.

Setup row (RS): K4, sm, yo, k to last 4 sts, yo, sm, k4—98 sts.

Next row (WS): K4, sm, p to next m, sm, k4.

Rep these 2 rows 8 more times then break off color A, switching to color B—114 sts.

Row 1 (transition row—RS): K4, sm, yo, k1, *sl 1, k1, rep from * to last st before m, k1, yo, sm, k4—116 sts.

Row 2 (WS): K4, sm, p to next m, k4.

Row 3: K4, pm, yo, k to last 3 sts, yo, pm, k4—118 sts.

Row 4: K4, sm, p to next m, sm, k4.

Work rows 3 and 4 three more times—124 sts.

Switch to color C and work rows 1–4 then work rows 3 and 4 six more times—140 sts.

Switch to color D and work rows 1–4, then work rows 3 and 4 six more times—156 sts.

Switch to color E and work rows 1–4, then work rows 3 and 4 four more times—168 sts.

Switch to color F and work rows 1–4, then work rows 3 and 4 six more times—184 sts.

Switch to color G and work rows 1–4, then work rows 3 and 4 three more times—194 sts.

Switch to color H and work rows 1–4, then work rows 3 and 4 one more time—200 sts.

Knit 6 rows, then BO all sts loosely.

Finishing:

Weave in all ends and gently steam-block.

DESIGNED BY *Deborah Stack*

Lombard Street Scarf

A simple chevron stitch serves as a fun background for bold stripes. By using a palette of rainbow-hued Bonbons, Chevron peaks mirror crayons in a box! Despite the complex look of this stitch pattern, it is easy to memorize and fun to knit.

SKILL LEVEL: Easy to Intermediate

Finished Measurements
68"/172cm long and 10.5"/27cm wide

Materials and Tools
> 3 packages of Lion Brand Bonbons in Crayons sport weight (100% acrylic; 24 x 0.35oz/10g, 28yd/26m each) —approx 672yd/614m
> Size 6 US (4mm) needles

Gauge
> 20 stitches/32 rows = 4"/10cm
> *Always take time to check your gauge.*

INSTRUCTIONS

Cast on 73 stitches.

Row 1 (RS): K1, yo, k4, s2kp, k4, *m1r, k1, m1l, k4, s2kp, k4. Rep from *4 times, yo, K1.

Row 2 (WS): Purl.

Rows 3–20: Repeat rows 1–2 nine times. Join new color. Continue to repeat rows 1–2, changing color every 20 rows, 24 times or until yarn runs out. *Note:* There will be 6 chevrons across the rows. Loosely bind off.

Finishing:

Wet-block, taking care to pin chevron points at either end of the scarf. Weave in ends.

Sideways Siberian Scarf

The perfect project for an absolute beginner, this scarf adds whimsy to your wardrobe, while perfecting your cast-on and bind-off skills. Adapt the pattern by adding more rows, changing the color sequence, or knitting it all with one color.

SKILL LEVEL: Easy

Finished Measurements:
One size
6"/15cm wide x 75"/190.5cm long

Materials and Tools
> Dragonfly Fibers Dragon Sock Gradient Set, shown in Siberian iris (100% superwash merino wool; 570yd/521m per six 1oz/28g skein set) —300yd/274m total fingering-weight yarn (*Note:* Approx 60yd/55m of each color were used.)
> Size 5 US (3.75mm) 40"/101.5cm long circular needle
> Large-eyed, blunt darning needle

Gauge
> 24 sts/24 rows = 4"/10cm in garter stitch
> *Always take time to check your gauge.*

INSTRUCTIONS:
Notes:
> If using a gradient set, take the time to label each individual skein A–E, or however many you use.
> A circular needle is used to accommodate a large number of stitches. Work back and forth in rows as if working with straight needles.

Cast on 430 sts in A.

Rows 1–3: Knit.

Row 4: Bind off 30 sts, knit to the end of the row. **Do not turn.** Break yarn, and with B, cast on 30 sts at the end of this row. After casting on, turn.

Rows 5–8: Knit.

Repeat rows 4–8, with the following sequence of colors: C, D, E, D, C, B, A.

On the final row, bind off all stitches.

Finishing:

With a darning needle, weave your ends through 10 purl bumps, and then stretch the scarf gently, before cutting each end. Block, and enjoy.

For the Hands, Legs & Feet

Matrix Mitts

Short mitts don't have to be dull. This variation on the traditional lice knitting pattern is an excellent introduction to colorwork.

SKILL LEVEL: Easy

Finished Measurements:
Small (Medium, Large):
Palm circumference approx 8″ (8.6″, 9.2″) /20 (22, 23)cm

Materials and Tools
> 2 (3) skeins Madelinetosh Unicorn Tails (100% superwash merino wool fingering-weight yarn; 52yd/48m): (MC), Edison bulb
> 1 skein Madelinetosh Unicorn Tails (100% superwash merino wool fingering-weight yarn; 52yd/48m): (CC1), silver fox
> 1 skein Madelinetosh Unicorn Tails (100% superwash merino wool fingering-weight yarn; 52yd/48m): (CC2), charcoal
> Size 3 US (3.25mm) double-pointed needles
> 3 stitch markers
> Stitch holder or spare yarn
> Tapestry needle

Gauge
> 26 sts/35 rows = 4″/10cm on size 3 US (3.25mm) needles in the round, post-blocking (*Note:* Keep tension and colorwork floats loose enough to allow the mitts to stretch.)
> *Always take time to check your gauge.*

INSTRUCTIONS

Mitts (make 2)

Rnd 1: With MC, cast on 48 (52, 56) stitches. Join to knit in the round, being careful not to twist the yarn. Place m to mark BOR.

Rnds 2–7: *K2, p2, rep from * around.

Rnd 8: Knit all sts.

Rnds 9–32: Work through chart 3 full times.

Begin Thumb Increases:

Rnd 33: Work rnd 1 of chart.

Rnd 34 (inc rnd): Working rnd 2 of chart, work 23 (25, 27) sts in pattern, pm, (kfb) twice, pm, work in pattern until end of rnd—50 (54, 58) sts (2 sts increased).

Rnd 35: Work the next rnd of the chart.

Rnd 36: Work the next rnd of the chart to the stitch marker, sm, kfb, work in patt to next marker, kfb, sm, work in patt—52 (56, 60) sts (2 sts increased).

Rnds 37–52: Rep rnds 35–36 eight more times, incorporating colorwork chart between markers when there are enough sts—68 (72, 76) sts (20 sts increased total).

Continue in patt (without increasing) until thumb depth is 2½" (2¾", 3") /6.5 (7, 7.5)cm or desired depth, ending with an even chart rnd.

Next rnd: Work in patt to marker, remove marker and work next st, place next 20 sts on spare yarn or stitch holder for thumb, CO 4 sts across thumb gap, then finish rnd in patt, removing remaining marker—52 (56, 60) sts.

Continue in patt 10 more rnds or until desired length.

Next 6 rnds: In MC only, *k2, p2, rep from * around.

Next rnd: Bind off in patt.

Thumb:

Place held stitches onto double-pointed needles. With MC, pick up and knit 4 sts across the thumb gap—24 sts. Join to knit in the round.

Rnds 1–6: *K2, p2, rep from * around.

Rnd 7: Bind off in patt.

Using tapestry needle, weave in ends. To even out stitches, block using your favorite technique.

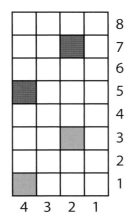

DESIGNED BY *Yelena M. Dasher*

Chevron Boot Toppers

The colors of the Southwest come together to make the perfect accessory for your cowboy—or any other style—boots.

SKILL LEVEL: Easy

Finished Measurements:
Small (Medium, Large)
13 (14½, 16)"/33 (37, 40.5)cm in circumference x 6½"/16.5cm tall

Materials and Tools

> Kim Dyes Yarn Superwash Merino wool in speckled eggs mini skeins (A-G), (A), vanilla ice cream; (B), soft pink; (C), mint chip; (D), banana cream; (E), soft persimmon; (F), robin's egg blue; (G), complementary brown 35yd/32m per mini) —245yd/224m total of 100% superwash merino wool DK weight yarn (*Note:* Seven different colors of any DK weight yarn will work, though I would suggest mostly wool for blends.)
> Two size 5 US (3.75mm) 24"/61cm circular needles (or preferred length for small-circumference knitting in the round, e.g., 16"/40.5cm circular needle, DPNs)
> Tapestry needle

Gauge

> 22 sts/32 rows = 4"/10.2cm in stockinette stitch
> *Always take time to check your gauge*

Stripe Sequence

> A, (B, C, D, E, F) twice, G.

INSTRUCTIONS

Cast on 72 (80, 88) with A stitches, pm (BOR), and join for working in the round.
Work 4 rnds in seed stitch.
Change to B.
Begin working from chart, knitting all stitches, and continue to change color as in Stripe Sequence.
Work the chevron chart until you have made 12 total chevrons vertically.
Work 4 rnds in seed stitch with G.
Bind off all stitches.
Weave in all ends, making sure to tightly close any gaps between stitches due to the color changes.

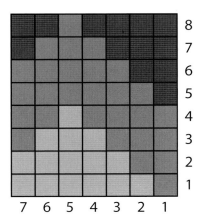

DESIGNED BY *Meg Roke*

French Ticking Fingerless Mitts

These simple and timeless fingerless mittens are inspired by the classic blue and white striping pattern found in traditional French ticking fabric.

SKILL LEVEL: Easy

Finished Measurements:

Approx circumference (at hand): 7"/18cm

Approx length (from bottom of cuff to top of hand): 10"/25.5cm

Materials and Tools

> Dream in Color in classy (100% superwash merino wool; 50yd/46m, 23g per mini skein): 1 mini skein in crying dove (MC) and 1 mini skein in midnight derby (CC) —worsted weight—or 50yd/46m of any worsted weight for MC and 50yd/46m of any worsted weight for CC

> Size 6 US (4mm) double-pointed needles or size needed to obtain gauge

> Stitch markers

> Waste yarn or stitch holder

> Scissors

> Tapestry needle

Gauge

> 19 sts/23 rows = 4"/10cm in stockinette stitch on size 6 US (4mm) needles

> *Always take time to check your gauge.*

INSTRUCTIONS

Stripe Sequence:

Work (1 rnd with MC, 2 rnds with CC) 3 times, 5 rnds with MC, (1 rnd with CC, 1 rnd with MC) twice, 13 rnds with CC, (1 rnd with MC, 1 rnd with CC) twice, 5 rnds with MC, (2 rnds with CC, 1 rnd with MC) twice, 1 rnd with CC.

Cuff:

With MC, CO 33 sts, divide sts evenly onto 3 double-pointed needles, pm, and join to work in the rnd.

Work in k2, p1 rib for 9 rnds.

Hand:

Work in stockinette stitch for the rest of the hand and at the same time, work through the Stripe Sequence or rnd 18 of the striping chart.

Thumb Gusset:

Rnd 19 (with CC): K1, pm, m1R, k1, m1L, pm, k to end—35 sts.

Rnd 20: Knit.

Rnd 21 (inc rnd): K1, sm, m1R, k to m, m1L, sm, k to end—37 sts.

Work next rnd even.

Rep last 2 rnds 4 more times (13 sts between markers) —45 sts total.

Next rnd (rnd 31 of chart): With CC, k1, remove marker, slip 13 sts onto waste yarn or stitch holder for thumb, remove marker, using the cable cast-on CO 1 st, k to end—33 sts.

Continue to work in stockinette stitch and at the same time continue to work through the rest of the striping chart.

With CC, BO.

Thumb:

Slip 13 sts from waste yarn back onto needles as follows: 5 sts on needle one, 5 sts on needle two, and 3 sts on needle three.

With MC and needle 3, pick up and knit 2 sts over the gap of the thumb gusset—15 sts total.

Knit 1 rnd even.

Work in k2, p1 rib for 5 rnds.

BO in rib pattern.

Finishing:

Weave in all ends.

Block to measurements.

☐	MC
■	CC

DESIGNED BY *Barbara J. Brown*

Mini Skein Knee Socks

Whether you purchase premade mini skeins, or just have odds and ends left over from your sock knitting, this pattern is a great—and colorful—way to make use of small amounts of fingering-weight yarn. A lovely panel with a leaf lace motif runs up the back of the leg, adding elegance and style.

SKILL LEVEL: Intermediate

Finished Measurements:

Small (Medium, Large):

Leg circumference at top: 11¼ (12¼, 13¼)"/28.5 (31, 33.5)cm

Leg height to top of heel: 15 (15, 15)"/38 (38, 38) cm

Foot circumference: 8 (9, 10)"/20.5 (23, 25.5)cm

Materials and Tools

> Ancient Arts Fibre 100% Superwash BFL Wool 4-Ply Fingering/Sock (100% superwash blue faced leicester; 437yds/400m per 3½oz/100g skein): (MC), 1 skein in color enchanted forest—or approx 400yd/365m of fingering-weight yarn

> Black Bunny Fibers Miniskeins Kit (100% superwash merino wool; total weight 100g = 400yd/365m): (CC), 1 kit (approx 4 mini skeins) of fingering-weight yarn

> Size 1 US (2.25mm) double-pointed needles or size needed to obtain gauge

> Stitch markers

> Stitch holder

> Tapestry needle

Gauge

> 32sts/40 rows = 4"/10cm using MC in stockinette stitch knit in the rnd

> *Always take time to check your gauge.*

INSTRUCTIONS (make 2 of each):

Cuff:

With the first CC, CO 87 (93, 99) sts. Join for working in the round, being careful not to twist the yarn, and dividing sts evenly among needles. Work 3 rnds of ribbing in the first color; work 2 rnds of ribbing in the next CC.

Rep these 5 rnds 2 more times, changing colors in the same manner—total of 15 ribbing rnds.

Next rnd: Do not change color; knit, inc 3 (5, 7) sts evenly around—90 (98, 106) sts.

Leg:

Switch to MC.

Next rnd: K38 (46, 54), pm, k31, pm, k to end.

Rnd 1: K to the first marker, sm, work the first round of the lace chart, sm, k to end.

Rnd 2: K to the first marker, sm, work the next consecutive round of the lace chart, sm, k to end.

Rnds 3–9: Rep rnd 2.

Rnd 10: K to 2 sts before m, k2tog, sm, work the next consecutive round of the lace chart, sm, ssk, k to end—88 (96, 104) sts.

Rep these 10 rnds, dec 2 sts on rnd 10 of each repeat, until 64 (72, 80) sts rem (25 [33, 41] sts before m, 31 sts, m, 8 sts).

Cont working lace chart, discontinuing dec on rnd 10 until sock measures 15"/38cm or desired length to top of heel flap, ending with a rnd 10.

Divide for Heel:

K24 (30, 36) and place these sts with the last 7 (5, 3) sts of the round on the holder for the instep.

Work Heel Flap on rem 33 (37, 41) sts.

Heel Flap (worked back and forth):

Note: Begin working Heel Flap with a mini skein and change mini skeins every 2 rows.

K across rem 33 (37, 41) sts, decr 1 sts—32 (36, 40) sts.

Row 1 (WS): Sl 1, k to end.

Row 2 (RS): Sl 1, *k1, slwyib, rep from * to last st, k1.

Row 3 (WS): Sl 1, k to end.

Work rows 2 and 3 only 15 (17, 19) more times.

Turn Heel:

Row 1 (RS): K16 (18, 20), ssk, k1, turn.

Row 2 (WS): Sl 1, p1, p2tog, p1, turn.

Row 3: Sl 1, k2, ssk, k1, turn.

Row 4: Sl 1, p3, p2tog, p1, turn.

Cont in this fashion, working one more st on each row before dec, until all sts have been worked, omitting the last st on the last 2 rows—16 (18, 20) Heel sts rem.

Break off mini skein and switch to CC for gusset and foot.

Gusset:

Next rnd: With needle 1, knit across 16 (18, 20) sts for heel, pick up and knit 16 (18, 20) sts along left side of Heel Flap; with needle 2, knit across 31 (35, 39) instep sts; with needle 3, pick up and knit 16 (18, 20) sts along right side of Heel Flap, knit across 8 (9) sts of heel. Place marker if desired to mark beg of rnd, which now begins at center of heel—79 (89, 99) sts (24 [27, 30] sts each on needles 1 and 3, and 31 [35, 39] sts on needle 2).

Rnd 1: Knit.

Rnd 2: Needle 1: K to last 3 sts, k2tog, k1. Needle 2: Knit. Needle 3: K1, ssk, k to end.

Rnd 3: Knit.

Rep rnds 2 and 3 until 63 (71, 79) sts rem.

Foot:

Work without further dec, keeping pattern correct, until foot measures 7 (8, 9)"/18 (20, 23) cm or 2"/5cm less than desired total length.

Toe:

Knit 1 rnd, dec 1 st on sole of foot—62 (70, 78) sts rem.

Break off MC and alternate mini skeins every 2 rnds or as desired.

Rnd 1: Needle 1: K to last 3 sts, k2tog, k1. Needle 2: K1, ssk, work in pattern to last 3 sts, k2tog, k1. Needle 3: K1, ssk, k to end of rnd.

Rnd 2: Knit.

Repeat rnds 1 and 2 until 18 (22, 22) sts rem. Graft toe using Kitchener st and weave in all ends. Block as desired.

Lace Chart (worked over 31 sts):

Rnd 1: K2, yo, k2tog, yo, k1, yo, k3, s2tog-k1-p2sso, k3, yo, s2tog-k1-p2sso, yo, k3, s2tog-k1-p2sso, k3, yo, k1, yo, ssk, yo, k2.

Rnd 2 and all even rnds: Knit.

Rnd 3: K2, yo, k2tog, yo, k3, yo, k2, s2tog-k1-p2sso, k2, yo, s2tog-k1-p2sso, yo, k2, s2tog-k1-p2sso, k2, yo, k3, yo, ssk, yo, k2.

Rnd 5: K2, yo, k2tog, yo, k5, yo, k1, s2tog-k1-p2sso, k1, yo, s2tog-k1-p2sso, yo, k1, s2tog-k1-p2sso, k1, yo, k5, yo, ssk, yo, k2.

Rnd 7: K2, yo, k2tog, yo, k7, (yo, s2tog-k1-p2sso) 3 times, yo, k7, yo, ssk, yo, k2.

Rnd 9: K2, yo, k2tog, yo, k8, k2tog, yo, s2tog-k1-p2sso, yo, ssk, k8, yo, ssk, yo, k2.

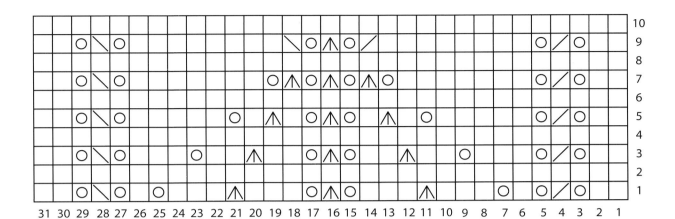

	knit
O	yo
/	k2tog
\	ssk
⋏	s2tog-k1-p2sso

Simple Sideways Mitts

Sometimes the simple things are the most visually pleasing. These mitts, designed specifically for absolute beginners, will add a gorgeous pop of color to your wardrobe. Become the designer, and mix up the pattern by alternating two colors, or go for crazy stripes and use up all those odds and ends you have lying around. You'll need only 6yd/5.5m for two rows.

SKILL LEVEL: Easy

Finished Measurements:

8.5"/21.5cm high x 7"/18cm in circumference (with about 1"/2.5cm of negative ease)

Materials and Tools

> GnomeAcres House Gnome (MC) (75% superwash merino wool, 25% nylon; 40yd/36.5m, 0.3oz/8.5g per skein); 3 skeins shown in cream—approx 110yd/100.5m in fingering-weight yarn

> Dragonfly Fibers Dragon Sock Gradient Set, shown in Siberian iris (A-E) (100% superwash merino wool; 95yd/87m, 1oz/28g per mini skein); 570yd/521m, 6oz/170g total—approx 30yd/27m total of fingering-weight yarn (*Note:* If using a gradient set, take the time to label each individual skein A-E, or however many you use.)

> Size 4 US (3.5mm) needles, straight or circular

> 2 stitch markers

> Large-eyed, blunt darning needle

Gauge

> 25 sts/32 rows = 4"/10cm in stockinette stitch

> *Always take time to check your gauge.*

INSTRUCTIONS

Left Hand:

With MC, cast on 53 sts.

Row 1 (RS): P15, pm, k33, pm, p5.

Row 2: K5, sm, p33, sm, k15.

Row 3: Knit.

Row 4: Purl.

Rows 5–32: Repeat rows 1–4 seven more times.

Rows 33–56: Repeat rows 1–4 six more times, changing color as in the following sequence: Work 2 rows with A, 2 rows with B, 2 rows with C, 2 rows with C, 2 rows with E and 14 rows with MC.

Bind off.

Right Hand:

Rows 1–12: Work as for left hand until row 12 is completed.

Rows 13–56: Repeat rows 1–4 of left hand 11 more times, changing color in the following sequence: Work 2 rows with E, 2 rows with D, 2 rows with C, 2 rows with B, 2 rows with A, and 34 rows with MC.

Bind off.

Finishing:

Turn each Sideways Mitt to the wrong side, and, with a darning needle, weave each loose end through about 10 purl bumps, give the work a slight stretch, then cut the yarn. With right sides together, whipstitch the side seam together from cuff edge to about 1"/2.5cm above the top of the cuff. Whipstitch down from the top of the mitten to about 3"/7.5cm from the top of the cuff, creating a gap for the thumb. Weave in the ends, and block.

DESIGNED BY *Susie Dippel*

Touch of Color Cabled Legwarmers

Reminiscent of stockings with the line down the back of the leg, these leg warmers have a touch of color along the cabling. The cables can be worn along the outside of the legs or the back of the legs. The tonal nature of Koigu handpainted yarn makes it seem as if more than three colors are used.

SKILL LEVEL: Intermediate

Finished Measurements:

12½"/32cm in circumference x 18"/45.5cm tall

Materials and Tools

> Koigu KPM (100% merino wool; 175 yd/160m): (MC), 3 skeins, color 1040 (teal) or 525 yd/480m of any fingering-weight yarn
> Koigu KPM (100% merino wool; approx 11 yd/10m): (A), 3 mini skeinettes color 1209 (ochre) or 33 yd/30.25m of any fingering-weight yarn
> Koigu KPM (100% merino wool; approx 11 yd/10m): (B), 3 mini skeinettes color 2424 (brown gray) or 33 yd/30.25m of any fingering-weight yarn
> Double-pointed needles: size 3 US (3.25mm) and size 4 US (3.5mm) or whatever size needles are needed to obtain gauge
> Cable needle that accommodates the larger needle
> Stitch markers
> Tapestry needle (to weave in ends)

Gauge

> 28 sts/32 rows = 4"/10cm in stockinette stitch, worked in rounds using larger needle
> *Always take time to check your gauge.*

Notes

> Dealing with more than one yarn in an area of knitting is called *intarsia*.
> Recognize that there is only one working yarn and other yarns are inactive.
> When the knitting is held in your hands, the yarns are on the back of the knitting.
> Wrap the working yarn around the inactive yarn; this secures the inactive yarn, prevents the appearance of holes, and keeps it close to the knitting.

In the case of this pattern, for every round:

> When the MC of the cable is being knit for the first time, wrap it around the main color.
> When color A is being knit for the first time, wrap it around the main color and the first color.

> When the cable stitches are done, wrap the main color around colors A and B and return to knitting the rest of the round with the main color.
> Remember to avoid tight stitches. Once on the RH needles, move around the intarsia stitches, spreading them out a bit.
> Every round (or every few rounds) disentangle the yarns. It will be easier to work with them in following rounds.

INSTRUCTIONS
Leg Warmer (make 2):

Using the larger needles and MC, cast on 88 stitches.

Divide stitches as follows: 30 stitches on needle one, 28 stitches on needle two, 30 stitches on needle three. Use a stitch marker (or another type of reminder) to indicate the beginning of the round.

Ribbing:
Change to the smaller needles.
Rnds 1–10: *K1, p1, rep from * around.
Rnd 11: Knit.

Two-Color Cable Section:
Change to larger needles.
Rnd 12: With MC, k38, p1, pm, pick up color A and k5, pick up color B and k5, pm, pick up color MC, p1, k38 to end the round.
Rnds 13–21: With MC, k38, p1, sm, with A, k5; with B, k5; with MC, p1, k38.
Rnd 22 (cable rnd): With MC, k38, p1, sm, slip the 5 color A sts onto a CN, let the CN dangle in front of your round; with B, knit the 5 color B sts from the left-hand needle; with A, knit the 5 color A sts from the CN; with MC, p1, k38.
Rnds 23–32: With MC, k38, p1, sm; with B, k5; with A, k5, sm; with MC, p1, k38.
Rnd 33 (cable rnd): With MC, k38, p1, sm; slip 5 color B sts onto a CN, let the CN dangle in front of your round; with A, knit the 5 color A sts from the left needle; with B, knit the 5 color B sts from the CN; with MC, p1, k38.
Repeat rnds 12–33 five more times, slipping markers as you come to them when working rnd 12 (instead of placing new markers).
Next rnd: Knit.

Ribbing:
Change to smaller needles.
Next 10 rnds: *K1, P1, rep from * around.
Using the larger needles, bind off loosely.

Finishing:
Weave in ends using the tapestry needle.
Block as needed.

DESIGNED BY *Barbara J. Brown*

Picture This! Socks

Looking at my collection of mini skeins, a picture of a rainbow appeared in my mind's eye. Try making this your own . . . a walk on the beach, sunrise on the prairies, a walk in the woods. The black used between the color changes helps to give these socks a coordinated look.

SKILL LEVEL: Intermediate

Finished measurements:
Small (Medium, Large):
Leg circumference: 7½ (8¼, 8¾)"/19 (21, 22)cm
Leg height to top of heel: 7"/18cm

Materials and Tools

> 7 different colors of Black Bunny Fibers Workhorse Wool Mini Skeins (100% superwash merino wool; 40g = 80yd/73m each) (*Note:* The pictured sample used colors red, orange, yellow, green, blue, purple, and black.)
> Size 1 US (2.25mm) double-pointed needles or size needed to obtain gauge
> Stitch markers
> Stitch holder
> Tapestry needle

Gauge

> 32 sts/40 rows = 4"/10cm using MC in stockinette stitch knit in the round
> *Always take time to check your gauge.*

INSTRUCTIONS (MAKE 2)

Cuff:

With first mini skein (red in sample) cast on 60 (64, 70) sts. Join for working in the round, being careful not to twist the yarn, and dividing sts evenly among needles.

Rnds 1–15: *K1, p1, rep from * to end of rnd.

Rnd 16 (inc rnd): Knit, inc 0 (1, 0) sts evenly around—60 (65, 70) sts.

Leg:

Change to black.

Rnd 1: *K4, sl 1 purlwise, rep from * around

Rnd 2: Knit.

Break black. Join second color (orange).

Rnd 3: *K4, sl 1 purlwise, rep from * around.

Rnd 4: *Yo, sl 1-k2tog-psso, p2, rep from * around.

Rnds 5–7: *K3, p2, rep from * around.

Rnds 8–15: Rep rnds 4–7 twice (3 complete repeats of lace chart).

Rnd 16: Knit.

Rep rnds 1–16 using yellow in place of orange.

Rep rnds 1–16 using green in place of orange.

Change to black.

Next rnd: Rep rnd 1.

Next rnd: Knit to last 1 (2, 3) sts, move the BOR marker here.

Divide for Heel:

Knit across first 30 (32, 34) sts and place on a holder for instep.

Work heel flap on rem 30 (33, 36) sts.

Heel Flap:

Change to purple.

Setup row: Knit, inc 0 (1, 0) sts—30 (34, 36) sts.

Row 1: Sl 1, purl to end.

Row 2: *Sl 1, k1, rep from * to end.

Rows 3–14 (16, 18): Rep rows 1 and 2.

Row 15 (17, 19): Rep row 1.

Shape Flap:

Row 1: [Sl 1, k1] 5 times, [sl 1] 0 (1, 1) time(s), k2tog, [k1, sl 1] 3 (4, 5) times, ssk, [k1] 0 (1, 1) time(s), [sl 1, k1] to end—28 (32, 34) sts.

Row 2: Sl 1, p to end.

Row 3: [Sl 1, k1] 4 (5, 5) times, [sl 1] 1 (0, 0) time(s), k2tog, [k1, sl 1] 3 (4, 5) times, ssk, [k1] 1 (0, 0) time(s), [sl 1, k1] to end—26 (30, 32) sts.

Row 4: Sl 1, p to end.

Row 5: Row 5: [Sl 1, k1] 4 times, [sl 1] 0 (1, 1) time(s), k2tog, [k1, sl 1] 3 (4, 5) times, ssk, [k1] 0 (1, 1) time(s), [sl 1, k1] to end—24 (28, 30) sts.

Row 6: Sl 1, p to end.

Row 7: [Sl 1, k1] 3 (4, 4) times, [sl 1] 1 (0, 0) time(s), k2tog, [k1, sl 1] 3 (4, 5) times, ssk, [k1] 1 (0, 0) time(s), [sl 1, k1] to end—22 (26, 28) sts.

Row 8: Sl 1, p to end.

Shape Heel:

Row 1: (RS) Sl 1, k13 (16, 17), ssk. Turn.

Row 2: (WS) Sl 1, p6 (8, 8), p2tog. Turn.

Row 3: (RS) Sl 1, k6 (8, 8), ssk. Turn.

Row 4: (WS) Sl 1, p6 (8 8), p2tog. Turn.

Continue in this fashion until all flap sts have been knit—8 (10, 10) sts remain.

Change to blue.

Setup for foot: With needle 1, k8 (10, 10) and with the same needle pick up 11 (12, 13) sts on the side

of the Heel Flap; with needle 2, work across the first 15 (16, 17) instep sts on holder; with needle 3, work across the remaining 15 (16, 17) insteps sts on holder; with needle 4, pick up 11 (12, 13) sts along the edge of the Heel Flap and work the first 4 (5, 5) sts on needle 1—60 (66, 70) sts (15 [17, 18] sts each on needles 1 and 4, 15 [16, 17] sts each on needles 2 and 3). Mark as BOR.

Foot:

Continue working in stockinette in rnds until foot measures 5½"/14cm less than total desired foot length.

Change to black.

Rnd 1: With black, *k4, sl 1, rep from * to last 4 (2, 2) sts, k4 (2, 2).

Change to green.

Rnd 2: With green, rep rnd 1.

Rnds 3–7: With green, knit.

Rep rnds 1–7 using yellow in place of green.

Rep rnds 1–7 using orange in place of green.

Rep rnds 1–7 using red in place of green.

Next rnd: With black, rep rnd 1.

Change to purple.

Next rnd: With purple, rep rnd 1.

Shape Toe:

Work toe with purple only.

Setup rnd:

Needle 1: Knit, dec 0 (1, 1).

Needles 2 and 3: Knit.

Needle 4: Knit, dec 0 (1, 1).

Note: There should now be 15 (16, 17) sts on each of the 4 needles.

Rnd 1 (dec rnd):

Needle 1: Work to last 3 sts, k2tog, k1.

Needle 2: K1, ssk, work to end.

Needle 3: Work to last 3 sts, k2tog, k1.

Needle 4: K1, ssk, complete round.

Rnd 2: Work even.

Repeat rnds 1 and 2 until 28 (32, 36) total sts remain.

Work dec rnd only until 16 (16, 20) sts remain.

Finishing:

With needle 4 work sts on needle 1–8 (8, 10) sts on needle 4.

Slip sts from needle 3 onto needle 2–8 (8, 10) sts on needle 2.

Holding two needles together, graft sts using Kitchener stitch.

Weave in ends.

●	●				4
●	●				3
●	●				2
●	●	○	⋏	○	1

☐	knit
⊡	p
⊙	yo
⋏	sl1-k2tog-psso

For the Body

DESIGNED BY *Yelena M. Dasher*

Rainbow Cardi

Ever wanted to wear a rainbow, but something held you back? This rainbow cardigan uses bright, fun rainbow stripes, in a decidedly grown-up way. Whether you choose a traditional ROYGBIV (red, orange, yellow, green, blue, indigo, violet) color scheme or a rainbow of your own design, this fun cardi will put a smile on your face.

SKILL LEVEL: Intermediate

Sizes: XS (S, M, L, 1X, 2X)

Finished Bust Measurements:

31½ (35, 38½, 42, 45½, 49)"/80 (89, 98, 106.5, 115.5, 124.5)cm

Materials and Tools

> Madelinetosh Tosh Merino Light (100% superwash merino wool; 420yd/384m): (MC), antique lace. Suggested yardage: 550 (605, 660, 725, 790, 850)yd/503 (553, 603, 663, 722, 777)m

> Madelinetosh Unicorn Tails (100% superwash merino wool; 52yd/47.5m, 1 skein of each color) (CC1-10 [11,12]). Suggested yardage: 45 (52, 60, 65, 70, 75)yd/41 (47.5, 55, 59.5, 64, 68.5)m each. (*Note*: Sizes 38½"/98cm and 42"/106.5cm may wish to have 11 colors or to repeat 2 of the 10 colors 3 times to have enough striping vertically; sizes 45½"/115.5cm and 49"/124.5cm may wish to have 12 colors for the same reason.)

Note: Any fingering-weight yarn with a majority wool content will work for this pattern, provided you can obtain gauge.

> Two size 4 US (3.5mm) 24"/61cm circular needles (or preferred length for large-circumference knitting in the round and preferred method for small-circumference knitting in the round, i.e., 16"/40.5cm circular needle, DPNs; instructions in the pattern assume knitting the sleeves on two circular needles)

> 6 (6, 6, 7, 7, 7) buttons, approximately ½"/13mm in diameter

> 4 stitch markers

> Waste yarn

Gauge

> 24 sts/34 rows = 4"/10cm in stockinette stitch

> *Always take time to check your gauge.*

INSTRUCTIONS

Beginning at neck, CO 76 (94, 114, 134, 148, 158) sts.

Row 1 (WS): P4 (6, 8, 10, 12, 14) for Right Front, pm p12 (16, 20, 24, 26, 26) for Right Sleeve, pm, p44 (50, 58, 66, 72, 78) for Back, pm, p12 (16, 20, 24, 26, 26) for Left Sleeve, pm, p4 (6, 8, 10, 12, 14) for Left Front.

Row 2 (RS): (K to 1 st before marker, m1L, k1, sm, k1, m1R) 4 times, knit to end—84 (102, 122, 142, 156, 166) sts.

Row 3: Purl.

Repeat last 2 rows 23 (25, 26, 28, 30, 32) more times; after the 10th repeat, begin working with the first CC and alternate stripes as follows: 4 rows CC, 4 rows MC, using each CC twice before switching to the next CC—268 (302, 330, 366, 396, 422) sts 28 (32, 35, 39, 43, 47) sts for each front, 60 (68, 74, 82, 88, 92) sts for each Sleeve, and 92 (102 112, 124, 134, 144) sts for back).

Row 50 (54, 56, 60, 64, 68) (last of the raglan inc repeats): K1, m1L (k to 1 st before marker, m1L, k1, sm, k1, m1R) 4 times, k to a st before end of row, m1R, k1—278 (312, 340, 376, 406, 432) sts (30 [34, 37, 41, 45, 49] sts for each front, 62 [70, 76, 84, 90, 94] sts for each Sleeve, and 94 [104, 114, 126, 136, 146] sts for Back). Continue making these increases to the front (the first m1L and the last m1R) on every RS row 17 (19, 20, 21, 22, 24) more times.

Next row (and all WS rows): Purl.

Divide for Body and Sleeves:

Row 52 (56, 58, 62, 66, 70): K1, m1L, k to first marker, place next 62 (70, 76, 84, 90, 94) sts on waste yarn, remove marker, k to next marker, place next 62 (70, 76, 84, 90, 94) sts on waste yarn, remove marker, k to 1 st before end of row, m1R, k1—31 (35, 38, 42, 46, 50) sts on each front, 94 (104, 114, 126, 136, 146) sts on the back, and 154 (172, 188, 208, 226, 244) sts on the needle. Work as established (including the increases on the fronts every RS row) until the piece measures 3 (3¼, 3½, 3¾, 4, 4¼)"/7.5 (8, 9, 9.5, 10, 11)cm.

Waist Shaping:

Decrease row: (Work to 3 sts before marker, ssk, k1, sm, k1, k2tog) 2 times, work to end.

Work 11 rows.

Repeat last 12 rows 3 *more* times.

Work 15 rows.

Increase row: (K to 1 st before marker, m1R, k1, sm, k1, m1L) 2 times, k to end.

Work 11 rows.

Repeat last 12 rows 2 *more* times—186 (208, 226, 248, 268, 290) sts.

Continue to work in stockinette stitch. When you have finished with the final CC stripe, k 8 rows with MC. (For sizes 35"/89cm, 42"/106.5cm, and 45½"/115.5cm, dec 2 sts evenly on the final row of stockinette.)

Ribbing: (K2, p2) to last two stitches, k2.

Continue in 2x2 ribbing for 15 *more* rows.

BO in pattern.

Sleeves:

Starting at center underarm, pick up and knit 2 sts, then k across the 62 (70, 76, 84, 90, 94) held sts, pick up and knit 2 sts from right underarm, place BOR marker, joining to work in the round—66 (74, 80, 88, 94, 98) sts.

Knit 7 rounds. Match the CC and MC alternating to the body.

Decrease rnd: K1, k2tog, k to last 3 sts, ssk, k1— 64 (72, 78, 86, 92, 96) sts.

Knit 8 rnds.

Repeat last 9 rnds 12 more times—40, (48, 54, 62, 68, 72) sts.

Continue to work in stockinette stitch. When you have finished with the final CC stripe, knit 8 rounds with MC. (For sizes 38½"/98cm and 42"/106.5cm, dec 2 sts evenly on the final row of stockinette.)

Work 16 rounds in k2, p2 ribbing.

BO in pattern.

Collar and Button Band:

Pick up and knit 2 for every 3 stitches along the fronts and sides of the V-neck; pick up 1 stitch for each stitch along the back (make sure to have a multiple of 4 sts + 2 total sts, starting and ending with the same type of stitch).

Row 1: (P2, k2) to last 2 sts, p2.

Row 2: (K2, p2) to last 2 sts, k2.

Row 3: Rep row 1.

Row 4: K2, (p1, yo, k2tog, k1, [p2, k2] 3 times) 6 (6, 6, 7, 7, 7) times, work in established rib to end.

Row 5: Rep row 1, knitting the yarn overs as you come to them.

Row 6: Rep row 2.

Rows 7 and 8: Rep rows 1 and 2.

BO in pattern.

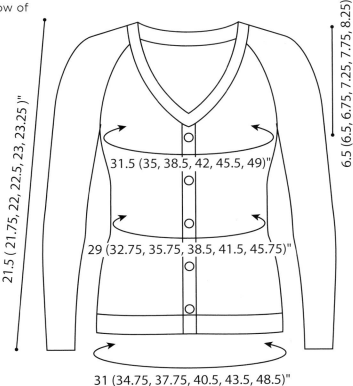

21.5 (21.75, 22, 22.5, 23, 23.25)"

6.5 (6.5, 6.75, 7.25, 7.75, 8.25)"

31.5 (35, 38.5, 42, 45.5, 49)"

29 (32.75, 35.75, 38.5, 41.5, 45.75)"

31 (34.75, 37.75, 40.5, 43.5, 48.5)"

DESIGNED BY *Yelena M. Dasher*

A Mermaid Darkly

Playing with multiple colors can be intimidating. This classic sweater uses a consistent color scheme to ease the wearer into the fun of knitting with many colors. Of course, any set of colors can be used; imagination is the only limitation!

SKILL LEVEL: Intermediate

Finished Bust Measurements:
30 (33, 36, 39, 42, 45, 48, 51)"/76 (84, 91.5, 99, 106.5, 114.5, 122, 129.5)cm

Materials and Tools

> Madelinetosh Tosh Merino Light (100% superwash merino wool): (MC1), ink—or 420yd/384m of fingering-weight yarn

> Madelinetosh Tosh Merino Light (100% superwash merino wool): (MC2), dirty panther —or 420yd/384m of fingering-weight yarn

> Orange Flower Merino Singles in mini skein set (100% single-ply merino) (CC1–7) —100yd/91m per mini skein of fingering-weight yarn

> Two size 3 US (3.25mm) 24"/61cm circular needles (or preferred length for large-circumference knitting in the round and preferred method for small-circumference knitting in the round, i.e., 16"/40.5cm circular needle, DPNs; instructions in the pattern assume knitting the sleeves on two circular needles)

> Stitch holders

> Tapestry needle

> MC1: 450 (500, 560, 590, 630, 675, 720, 765) yd/411 (457, 512, 539.5, 576, 617, 658, 700)m

> MC2: 280 (310, 340, 365, 390, 420, 450, 475) yd/256 (283, 310, 334, 356.5, 384, 411.5, 434.5)m

> CC1–7: 75 (80, 90, 95, 100, 110, 115, 120)yd/68.5 (73, 82, 87, 91.5, 100.5, 105, 110)m
Note: Any fingering-weight yarn with a majority wool content will work for this pattern, provided you can obtain gauge. I prefer the single-ply yarns for this design because of their depth of color.

Gauge

> 26 sts/36 rows = 4"/10cm in stockinette stitch

> Always take time to check your gauge.

NOTES:

This sweater is knit from the top down, first in pieces, and then in the round as follows: Start by knitting the Back Right Shoulder, followed by the Back Left Shoulder; the two shoulders are then joined when you add the stitches across the back neckline. Work the back of the sweater to the underarms. Pick up the stitches for the front of the sweater from the tops of each shoulder, one at a time. Start by picking up and knitting the Front Left Shoulder, followed by the Front Right Shoulder; the two shoulders are then joined when you add the stitches across the Front Neckline. Work the front of the sweater to the underarms. Then join the front and the back of the sweater when you add the underarm stitches and work the remainder of the sweater in the round. Sleeve stitches are picked up around the armholes and shaped with short-row sleeve caps before working the remainder of the sleeves in the round.

INSTRUCTIONS

Right Back Shoulder:

With MC1, cable cast-on 22 (23, 24, 26, 27, 28, 29, 30) sts.

Row 1: Purl.

Row 2 (RS): Knit.

Row 3: Purl.

Row 4: K10, wrap and turn.

Row 5: Purl.

Row 6: K1, m1L, k to end, picking up wrap—23 (24, 25, 27, 28, 29, 30, 31) sts.

Row 7: Purl.

Put stitches on holder.

Left Back Shoulder:

With MC1, cable cast-on 22 (23, 24, 26, 27, 28, 29, 30) sts.

Row 1: Purl.

Row 2 (RS): Knit.

Row 3: P10, wrap and turn.

Row 4: Knit.

Row 5: P, picking up wrap.

Row 6: K to last stitch, m1R, k1—23 (24, 25, 27, 28, 29, 30, 31) sts.

Row 7: Purl.

Join Shoulders:

Knit 23 (24, 25, 27, 28, 29, 30, 31) sts of Left Back Shoulder, cable cast on 39 (39, 43, 43, 46, 48, 52, 54) sts, knit the 23 (24, 25, 27, 28, 29, 30, 31) sts you put on hold for the Right Back Shoulder—85 (87, 93, 97, 102, 106, 112, 116) sts.

Work 46 (40, 40, 38, 36, 36, 36, 34) rows in stockinette.

Increase row: K1, m1R, k to last stitch, m1L, k1—86 (88, 94, 98, 103, 107, 113, 117) sts.

Next row: Purl.

Repeat those 2 rows 3 (7, 8, 11, 13, 16, 17, 20) more times—93 (103, 111, 121, 130, 140, 148, 158) sts.

Put stitches on holder.

Left Front Shoulder:

With RS facing and MC1, pick up and knit 22 (23, 24, 26, 27, 28, 29, 30) stitches across top of Left Back Shoulder.

Row 1: Purl.

Row 2 (RS): Knit.

Row 3: Purl.

Repeat rows 2 and 3 four more times.

Increase row: K1, m1R, k to end.

Next row: Purl.

Repeat last 2 rows 2 times—25 (26, 27, 29, 30, 31, 32, 33) sts.

Put stitches on holder.

Right Front Shoulder:

With RS facing and MC1, pick up and knit 22 (23, 24, 26, 27, 28, 29, 30) stitches across top of Right Back Shoulder.

Row 1: Purl.

Row 2 (RS): Knit.

Row 3: Purl.

Repeat rows 2 and 3 four more times.

Increase row: K1, m1R, k to end.

Next row: Purl.

Repeat last 2 rows 2 times—25 (26, 27, 29, 30, 31, 32, 33) sts.

Join Shoulders:

K 25 (26, 27, 29, 30, 31, 32, 33) sts of Right Front Shoulder, cable cast-on 35 (35, 39, 39, 42, 44, 48, 50) sts, k the 25 (26, 27, 29, 30, 31, 32, 33) stitches you put on hold for the Left Front Shoulder—85 (87, 93, 97, 102, 106, 112, 116) sts. Work 36 (30, 30, 28, 26, 26, 26, 24) rows in stockinette.

Increase row: K1, m1R, k to last stitch, m1L, k1—87 (89, 95, 99, 104, 108, 114, 118) sts.

Next row: Purl.

Repeat those two rows 3 (7, 8, 11, 13, 16, 17, 20) more times—93 (103, 111, 121, 130, 140, 148, 158) sts.

Join Front and Back:

Next row: Knit to end, CO 2 (2, 3, 3, 3, 3, 4, 4) sts, pm, CO 2 (2, 3, 3, 3, 3, 4, 4) sts, knit across back stitches from holder, CO 2 (2, 3, 3, 3, 3, 4, 4) sts, pm (BOR), CO 2 (2, 3, 3, 3, 3, 4, 4) sts—194 (214, 234, 254, 272, 292, 312, 332) sts.

You are now working in the round.

Knit 2 rounds.

Begin striping pattern. Stripes are worked 16 rounds in each contrast color, 2 rounds in MC1. You will decrease and increase within both colors. Continue in stripe pattern until you have striped with each contrast color and made a final MC1 stripe. All rounds after the last MC1 stripe will be in stockinette with MC2.

Work 2½ (3, 3, 3½, 3½, 3½, 4, 4)"/6.5 (7.5, 7.5, 9, 9, 9, 10, 10)cm in stockinette.

Next rnd: *K2tog, k to 2 sts before marker, ssk, sm; repeat from * once more—190 (210, 230, 250, 268, 288, 308, 328) sts.

Knit 6 (4, 4, 4, 4, 4, 4) rnds.

Repeat 7 (5, 5, 5, 5, 5, 5) previous rnds 7 (7, 8, 8, 7, 7, 7, 7) more times 8 (8, 9, 9, 8, 8, 8, 8 total dec rnds) —162 (182, 198, 218, 240, 260, 280, 300) sts.

Work 16 (20, 20, 16, 20, 20, 16, 16) rnds.

Next rnd: *K1, m1L, k to one st before marker, m1R, k1, sm; repeat from * once more—166 (186, 202, 222, 244, 264, 284, 304) sts.

Knit 4 (4, 3, 4, 4, 4, 4, 4) rnds.

Repeat 5 (5, 4, 5, 5, 5, 5, 5) previous rnds 5 (5, 9, 6, 5, 5, 5, 5) more times (6, 6, 10, 7, 6, 6, 6, 6 total inc rnds)—186, 206, 238, 246, 264, 284, 304, 324) sts.

Continue in pattern until length from underarm is 15 (16, 17, 18, 19, 20, 21, 22)"/38 (40.5, 43, 45.5, 48, 51, 53.5, 56)cm or 2"/5cm less than desired length.

Change to 2x2 ribbing for 16 rounds, continue using MC2.

Bind off in pattern.

Sleeves:

Starting in the center of the underarm, pick up and knit 70 (76, 80, 88, 94, 98, 106, 112) sts, placing a midpoint marker after stitch 35 (38, 40, 44, 47, 49, 53, 56) and one to indicate BOR.

Sleeve cap row 1: K to 11 (13, 14, 15, 16, 17, 18, 19) past midpoint marker, w+t.

Row 2: P (22, 26, 28, 30, 32, 34, 36, 38) sts, w+t.

Row 3: K to wrapped stitch, knit stitch with its wrap, w+t.

Row 4: P to wrapped stitch, purl stitch with its wrap, w+t.

Repeat rows 3 and 4 until 3 (3, 4, 4, 4, 4, 5, 5) sts remain on each side that have not been wrapped.

Dec row: Knit to wrapped stitch, ssk, k to end 2 (2, 3, 3, 3, 3, 4, 4) more stitches; you will now be working the sleeves in the round—69 (75, 79, 87, 93, 97, 105, 111) sts.

Rnd 1: K 2(2, 3, 3, 3, 3, 4, 4), k2tog, k to end—68 (74, 78, 86, 92, 96, 104, 110) sts.

Knit 1 round.

Next row begins striping pattern to match the body (16 rnds in CC, followed by 2 rounds in MC1). AT THE SAME TIME begin decreases every 17 (16, 11, 9, 9, 8, 7, 7)th round as follows: k1, k2tog, k to last 3 sts, ssk, k1. Make a total of 8 (9, 9, 13, 14, 16, 18, 20) decreases and end up with 52 (56, 60, 60, 64, 64, 68, 72) sts on the needles.

Finish the final MC1 stripe and knit with the MC until Sleeve measures 20 (20½, 21, 22, 22, 22, 23, 23)"/51 (52, 53.5, 56, 56, 56, 58.5, 58.5)cm from beginning OR desired length minus 2"/5cm is reached.

Work in 2x2 ribbing for 16 rounds.

Bind off in pattern.

Collar:

Starting at the Right Shoulder seam, pick up and
knit 100 (104, 108, 112, 116, 120, 124, 128) sts evenly
around neck and join to work in the round.
Work in 2x2 ribbing for 7 rounds.
Bind off very loosely in pattern.

Finishing:

Weave in all ends and block sweater to desired
measurements.

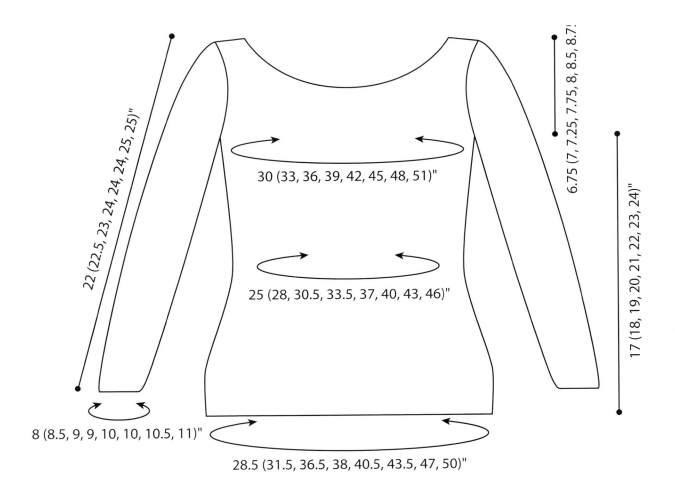

22 (22.5, 23, 24, 24, 24, 25, 25)"

6.75 (7, 7.25, 7.75, 8, 8.5, 8.7)

17 (18, 19, 20, 21, 22, 23, 24)"

30 (33, 36, 39, 42, 45, 48, 51)"

25 (28, 30.5, 33.5, 37, 40, 43, 46)"

8 (8.5, 9, 9, 10, 10, 10.5, 11)"

28.5 (31.5, 36.5, 38, 40.5, 43.5, 47, 50)"

For the Home

DESIGNED BY *Claire Cromwell*

Welcome Spring Oven Towel

Tired of having to hunt for a towel in the kitchen? Button this mitered one to your stove or fridge handle and you'll have a towel that is both decorative and useful!

SKILL LEVEL: Easy

Finished Measurements:
Approx 18½"/47cm tall (hanging strap unbuttoned) by 17"/43cm at widest point

Materials and Tools
> 1 package Lion Brand Bonbons in Nature sport weight (100% cotton, 0.35oz/10g, 28yd/26m per mini skein): (A), chocolate brown; (B), cream; (C), green; (D), tan; (E), dusty rose; (F), yellow; (G), palest lavender; (H), purple
> Size 3 US (3.25mm) needles
> Tapestry needle
> 2 buttons, ½"/13mm
> Sewing needle and thread

Gauge
> 28 sts/52 rows = 4"/10cm in garter stitch
> *Always take time to check your gauge.*

INSTRUCTIONS

With color A, CO 24 sts.

Work 6 rows in garter st.

Row 7 (buttonhole row): K4, k2tog, yo, knit to last 6 sts, yo, k2tog, k to end.

Continue in garter st until color A is used up, or until piece measures 5¼"/13cm from CO edge.

Begin Miter Shaping:

With color B, work the following rows once:

Setup row 1 (RS): Knit 11, m1, pm, k2, pm, m1, knit to end—26 sts.

Setup row 2: Knit.

Then work as follows:

Row 1: Knit to marker, m1, sm, k2, sm, m1, knit to end.

Row 2: Knit.

Rep last 2 rows until there are 60 sts on the needle, ending with a row 2.

Change to color C and rep rows 1 and 2 until there are 82 sts on the needle, ending with a row 2.

Change to color D and rep rows 1 and 2 until there are 100 sts on the needle, ending with a row 2.

Change to color E and rep rows 1 and 2 until there are 114 sts on the needle, ending with a row 2.

Change to color F and rep rows 1 and 2 until there are 126 sts on the needle, ending with a row 2.

Change to color G and rep rows 1 and 2 until there are 138 sts on the needle, ending with a row 2.

Change to color H and rep rows 1 and 2 until there are 148 sts on the needle, ending with a row 2.

Finishing:

Bind off.

Weave ends in and block.

With sewing thread and needle, sew buttons on approximately ¾"/2cm up from the border between colors A and B and ¾"/2cm in from the edge, 1¼"/3cm apart.

DESIGNED BY *Claire Cromwell*

Waffle Coasters

Add a cute vintage touch to your table with these cheerful coasters! Tied with some extra yarn and paired with a package of tea or coffee, they make a great hostess gift.

SKILL LEVEL: Easy

Finished Measurements:

4¼" x 4"/11cm x 10cm

Materials and Tools

> 1 package Lion Brand Bonbons in Beachsport weight (100% cotton; 0.35oz/10g, 28yd/26m per mini skein): in turquoise, orange, white, seafoam green, red, purple, black, yellow
> Size 4 US (3.5mm) needles
> Tapestry needle

Gauge

> 32 sts/60 rows = 4"/10cm) in slip stitch pattern
> *Always take time to check your gauge.*

Notes:

> One package of Bonbons is sufficient to make 8 coasters if each color is used once as color A and once as color B.
> Unless otherwise stated, stitches should be slipped with yarn in back.

INSTRUCTIONS

With color A, CO 32 sts.

Knit 1 row.

Row 1: With color B, sl 1, *k2, sl next 2 sts, rep from * to last 3 sts, end with k2, sl 1.

Row 2: Sl 1, *knit 2, sl 2 wyif, rep from * to last 3 sts, end with k2, sl 1 wyif.

Row 3: With color A, k1, *sl 2, k2, rep from * to last 3 sts, end with sl 2, k1.

Row 4: K1, *sl 2 wyif, k2, rep from * to last 3 sts, end with sl 2 wyif, k1.

Row 5: Work as row 1.

Row 6: Work as row 2.

Row 7: With color A, knit.

Row 8: Knit.

Repeat last 8 rows 7more times.

With color A, bind off.

Finishing:

Weave ends in.

Block to measurements.

DESIGNED BY

Chevron Coffee Cozy: Two Ways

Protect your hands and the earth with this cute cozy! Try making it in cotton for iced drinks in the summer, or use up all your scraps and knit a new cozy for every day of the week.

SKILL LEVEL: Easy

Finished Measurements:
3"/7.5cm tall x 8"/20.5cm in circumference
(will fit a 16oz/454g paper cup)

Materials and Tools
> 1 package Lion Brand Bonbons in Celebrate sport weight (96% acrylic, 4% metallic polyester, 0.35oz/10g, 38.3yd/35m per mini skein): (A), dark blue; (B), light blue; (C), emerald; (D), pea green; (E), purple; (F), hot pink; (G), red; (H) sparkling peach
> Size 3 US (3.25mm) needles
> Tapestry needle

Gauge
> 28 sts/38 rows = 4"/10cm in stockinette stitch
> *Always take time to check your gauge.*

Options
> Version 1: dark blue (A), light blue (B), emerald (C), pea green (D)
> Version 2: purple (E), hot pink (F), red (G), sparkling peach (H)

Stripe Pattern

4 rows A (E)	4 rows C (G)
2 rows B (F)	2 rows D (H)
2 rows A (E)	2 rows C (G)
4 rows B (F)	4 rows D (H)
2 rows C (G)	2 rows A (E)
2 rows B (F)	2 rows D (H)

INSTRUCTIONS
With A (E), CO 25 sts.
Purl 1 row.
Begin Chevron Stripe Pattern:
Row 1 (RS): K1, ssk, k9, yo, k1, yo, k9, k2tog, k1.
Row 2 (WS): Purl all sts, working yarn overs through the back loop.
Rows 3–64: Rep rows 1 and 2 and continue to change color as in Stripe Pattern until pattern has been repeated a total of 2 times.
Change to color A (E) and work rows 1 and 2 once more.
Bind off.

Finishing:
Weave ends in.
Block to measurements.
Seam short ends together using mattress stitch.

Square Pillow

Show off even the smallest scraps of yarn with this pillow. Use the recommended striping pattern or make up your own for a totally unique and comfortable decorative accent! We used neutrals on one side of our pillow and bright pastels on the flip side to give a completely new look and feel to a room in seconds.

SKILL LEVEL: Easy

Finished Measurements:
14" x 14"/35.5cm x 35.5cm

Materials and Tools
> 3 packages of Lion Brand Bonbons in Nature sport weight (100% cotton; 24 x 0.35oz/10g, 28yd/26m each): (A), approx 1 bonbon, cream; (B) approx 3 bonbons, tan; (C), approx 2 bonbons, lightest yellow; (D), approx 1 bonbon, dusty rose; (E), approx 3 bonbons, purple; (F), approx 2 bonbons, palest lavender—approx 672yd/614.5m total
> Two size 4 US (3.5mm), 16"/40.5cm circular needles
> Size 4 US (3.5mm) double-pointed needles
> 14"/35.5cm square machine-washable pillow form
> Stitch markers

Gauge
> 18 sts/32 rows = 4"/10cm in stockinette stitch
> *Always take time to check your gauge.*

INSTRUCTIONS

Side:

With color A, cast on 4 stitches across double-pointed needles. Join in the round, being sure not to twist your stitches. (*Note:* This pattern is also well-suited to the magic loop technique.)

Rnd 1 (RS): Knit.

Rnd 2 (RS): Kfbf in each st across row—12 sts.

Rnd 3: Knit.

Rnd 4: Place marker to indicate beginning of round. *K1, yo, pm, k1, pm, yo, k2, yo, pm, k1, pm, yo, k1 repeat from * once more—20 sts (8 markers placed).

Rnd 5: Purl.

Rnd 6: *Knit to marker, yo, sm, k1, sm, yo, knit to marker, repeat from * to end—28 sts.

Rnd 7: Purl.

Repeat rows 6 and 7 seven more times, transferring to circular needle when piece has grown large enough to comfortably fit—84 sts.

Cut color A. Join color B.

Repeat rows 6 and 7 six times—132 sts.

Cut color B. Join color C.

Repeat rows 6 and 7 seven times—188 sts.

Cut color C. Join color B.

Repeat rows 6 and 7 seven times—244 sts.

Set piece aside.

Repeat instructions for side 2, using alternate colors if desired—244 sts.

Finishing:

Once both sides of pillow are complete, weave in all ends. Line up both pieces of fabric, wrong sides together. Make sure to match beginning of row on both sides. Ensure that tips of both circular needles line up.

Using a double-pointed needle, perform a 3-needle bind-off around 3sides of pillow cover. Once pillow cover has only one open side, insert pillow form.

Complete 3-needle bind-off across remaining stitches, enclosing pillow form within knitted cover. Weave in any remaining ends.

DESIGNED BY *Barbara J. Brown*

Lydia Evening Bag

This is a vintage stitch from an old counterpane pattern. The scallop edge adds a touch of whimsy. Knit it in a painted yarn, as here, or use a single solid. Try it in ombre colors for a touch of fun. A vintage button is used to close.

SKILL LEVEL: Intermediate

Finished Measurements
7"/18cm long x 3½"/9cm high

Materials and Tools
> 1 mini skein Koigu KPPM fingering weight (100% merino wool; 175yd/160m; approx. 25yd/23m used)
> Size 1 US (2.25mm) needles or size needed to obtain gauge
> Stitch markers
> Tapestry needle
> 1 button, 1"/2.5cm diameter

Gauge
> 32 sts/40 rows = 4"/10cm in stockinette stitch
> *Always take time to check your gauge.*

INSTRUCTIONS

Cast on 52 sts.

Front Flap:

Note: Work flap by following written instructions or by working from Lydia chart

Row 1 (RS): *(K2, p2) 3 times, (kfbfbf) twice, (p2, k2) 3 times, repeat from * once more—68 sts.

Row 2: *P2, k2tog, p2, k2, p2, k14, p2, k2, p2, k2tog, p2, repeat from * once more—64 sts.

Row 3: *K2, p1, k2, p2, k2, p14, k2, p2, k2, p1, k2, repeat from * once more.

Row 4: *P2, k2tog, p1, k2, p2, k2, p10, k2, p2, k2, p1, k2tog, p2, repeat from * once more—60 sts.

Row 5: *K2, p1, ssk, p1, k2, p2, k10, p2, k2, p1, k2tog, p1, k2, repeat from * once more—56 sts.

Row 6 (buttonhole row): P2, k2tog, k1, p2, k2, p10, k2, p2, k1, k2tog, p1, k2tog, yo, p1, k2tog, k1, p2, k2, p10, k2 p2, k1, k2tog, p2—52 sts.

Rows 7–11: Repeat rows 1–5.

Row 12: *P2, k2tog, k1, p2, k2, p10, k2, p2, k1, k2tog, p2, repeat from * once more—52 sts.

Rows 13–18: Repeat rows 7–12.

Main Body:

Row 1: K2, p2, k2, *p1, k1, repeat from * to last 6 sts, k2, p2, k2.

Row 2: P2, k2, p2, *k1, p1, repeat from * to last 6 sts, p2, k2, p2.

Repeat rows 1 and 2 for 7"/18cm, ending with a wrong-side row.

Next Row: (K2tog) 3 times, knit to last 6 sts, (k2tog) 3 times—46 sts.

Border:

Row 1: Purl.

Rows 2 and 3: Knit.

Row 4: Purl.

Rows 5–7: Repeat rows 2–4.

Bind off.

Finishing:

Fold Main Body section in half, folding Border up to just below Front Flap, and sew side seams.

Sew button to match buttonhole.

Weave in ends, wash, and block as desired.

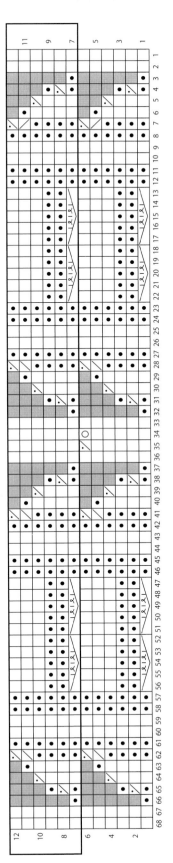

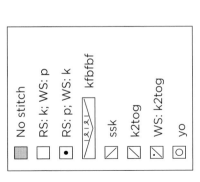

▨	No stitch
☐	RS: k; WS: p
•	RS: p; WS: k
⟋⟍	kfbfbf
⟋	ssk
⟍	k2tog
⟋•	WS: k2tog
○	yo

Abbreviations

approx	approximate(ly)
beg	begin/beginning
BO	bind off
BOR	beginning of round
CC	contrast color
cm	centimeter(s)
CN	cable needle
CO	cast on
cont	continue
dec/decr	decreas(e)(ing)
dpn	double pointed needle(s)
EOR	end of round
g	gram
inc/incr	increas(e)(ing)
k or K	knit
k1tbl	knit 1 stitch through the back loop
k2tog	knit two together
Kfb	Knit into the front and back of the next stitch
kfbf	Knit into the front, back, and then front again of the next stitch
kfbfbf	Knit into the front, back, front, back, and front again of the next stitch
LH	left hand
m1	make 1 (1 st increase)
m1L	make one left
m1R	make one right
m	marker
MC	main color
mm	millimeters
OTN	on the needle(s)
oz	ounce(s)

p or P	purl
patt	pattern
p1tbl	purl 1 stitch through the back loop
P2tog	purl the next two stitches together
Pfb	purl into the front and back of the next stitch
pm	place marker
PU	Pick up sts knitwise
rem	remain(ing)
rep	repeat
RH	right hand
rm	remove marker
rnd(s)	round(s)
RS	right side
s2tog-k1-p2sso	slip 2 together, knit 1, pass the 2 slipped sts over
sl	slip
sm	slip marker
sl m	slip marker
sl1-k2tog-psso	slip 1, knit 2 together, pass the slipped st over (2 sts decreased)
ssk	slip, slip, knit
st(s)	stitch(es)
stst	stockinette stitch
tbl	through back loop
tog	together
w+t	wrap and turn
WS	wrong side
wyib	with yarn in back
wyif	with yarn in front
yo	yarn over

Yarn Weight Chart

YARN WEIGHT SYMBOL + CATEGORIES	LACE **0**	SUPER FINE **1**	FINE **2**	LIGHT **3**	MEDIUM **4**	BULKY **5**	SUPER BULKY **6**	JUMBO **7**
TYPE OF YARNS IN CATEGORY	Fingering, 10-count crochet thread	Sock, Fingering, Baby	Sport, Baby	DK, Light, Worsted	Worsted, Afghan, Aran	Chunky, Craft, Rug	Super Bulky, Roving	Jumbo, Roving

Source: Craft Yarn Council of America's www.yarnstandards.com

Needle Conversion Chart

METRIC (MM)	U.S.	METRIC (MM)	U.S.
2	0	5.5	9
2.25	1	6	10
2.5	1	6.5	10½
2.75	2	7	10½
3	3	8	11
3.25	3	9	13
3.5	4	10	15
3.75	5	12	17
4	6	15	19
4.25	6	19	35
4.5	7	20	36
5	8	25	50

Yarn Resources

ANCIENT ARTS FIBRE
Ancientartsfibre.com

ASTRAL BATH YARN
etsy.com/shop/astralbath

BLACK BUNNY FIBERS
Blackbunnyfibers.com

COLOUR ADVENTURES
etsy.com/shop/ColourAdventures

THE COPPER CORGI
etsy.com/shop/TheCopperCorgi

DRAGONFLY FIBERS
Dragonflyfibers.com

DREAM IN COLOR
Dreamincoloryarn.com

GNOMEACRES
Gnomeacres.com

JULIE ASSELIN
julie-asselin.com/en

KIM DYES YARN
etsy.com/shop/KimDyesYarn

KOIGU
Koigu.com

LION BRAND
Lionbrand.com

MADELINETOSH
Madelinetosh.com

ORANGE FLOWER YARN
Orangefloweryarn.com

WESTERN SKY KNITS
Westernskyknits.com

About the Designers

Barbara J. Brown is a designer, lifelong knitter, Design Coordinator for Ancient Art Fibres, and lives in Alberta, Canada. She's the author of *Knitting Knee-Highs: Sock Styles from Classic to Contemporary* and her designs have appeared in *Vogue Knitting*, *Koigu Magazine*, and *The Knitter* (UK). She is very interested in the knitting traditions of all countries and in teaching these techniques to others. Many of her designs incorporate the unique stitches of these traditions. She is also involved in other aspects of the fiber world, including spinning, felting, and dyeing.

Holly Chayes is a fiber artist and designer who focuses on creating things with lace and color. Based in New York City, she has a background in costume design and an affinity for luscious fabrics, coffee, and the color black. You can find her writing about making things and handmade style at hollychayes.com.

Claire Cromwell learned to knit at the ripe old age of eighteen, upon seeing her sister learn and thinking,"That looks like fun." After a detour into hideous scarves, she now enjoys knitting sweaters, accessories, and all manner of cute nerdy things. Claire lives in Brooklyn with her husband and an ever-growing stash.

Yelena M. Dasher is in love with sweater knitting and in love with sweaters that look just as good with a blazer and skirt as they do with jeans. She designs sweaters with the modern, stylish, working (in the office or at home) woman in mind, and wants women to feel good about the way they look in their handknits. If you'd like to see how Yelena's own sweaters get worn (and get more than an occasional tip about a hot clothing sale), visit her blog at lepulljuste.blogspot.com. You can find her on Ravelry as ymalcolm.

Susie Dippel owns the online pattern and yarn business, Chiagu (chiagu.com). After a career in information technology, she is doing what most knitters dream about. Her favorite workday involves designing knitwear or curating colors for Chiagu's Koigu Mini Skein Club. In the future she looks forward to designing patterns for crochet, quilting, and sewing.

Dana E. Freed, in partnership with her mother, Bert Rachel Freed, is the founder and owner of the Well Done Experience. Through this outlet she shares her expertise and love for handcrafts through teaching, producing specialty DIY kits, and publishing her original designs (welldoneexperience.com). Dana and Bert's line of one-of-a-kind couture beadwork, Chicken & the Egg Designs, is sold in boutiques, galleries, and museums (chicken-egg.com). They are the authors of *Bead Crochet Jewelry: An Inspired Journey Through 27 Designs*.

Jess Kallberg believes that knitting (and wearing knitwear) should never be boring. She loves to pair traditional techniques with modern styling to create fashionable knits that can't be bought in a store. Jess brings her love of DIY to work at a craft technology startup in Brooklyn. You can find her on Ravelry as edifyarcane.

Meg Roke is a knitwear designer who, after working many years as a special education teacher, put teaching aside to stay home with her children. Over the last few years, she has branched out into designing knitwear and has a growing portfolio of online and print published designs. In her very rare spare time, she tries to squeeze in any quantity of knitting. She also enjoys gardening, baking, and sewing, in addition to watching way too much *Masterpiece Mystery!* and old movies. You can find her patterns on Ravelry, Etsy, and Craftsy and read about her crafting life on her blog: megrokeknits.blogspot.com.

Connie Santisteban is a craft book editor, knitter, yarn enthusiast, and shutterbug. She learned how to knit in order to have her own Harry Potter scarf in Hufflepuff house colors and from that moment on an avid knitter was born. She acquires yarn much faster than she can knit it, but can never say no to a perfect shade of kelly green. You can find her on Ravelry as lemontango and on Instagram as lemontangos.

Andi Smith has been knitting and stitching for longer than she can remember. She has been designing and teaching for nearly 10 years, and is currently working on a follow-up to her two-color cable e-book, *Synchronicity*. Andi is the author of *Big Foot Knits*, the e-book, *Synchronicity*, and can be found online as Knitbrit.

Deborah Stack is a serial hobbyist, but knitting will always be her one true love. In her spare time, she explores sewing and planning a rap-lyric embroidery series. If you find her at a party, she'll happily talk your ear off about the social and economic history of hand-knitting and its gendered implications. She is happiest with a project in her hands, and loves surprising and creative projects made with traditional crafts. Her workday is fueled by coffee and brightened by puns. If you see her knitting on the subway, make sure to say hello (as long as she's not counting stitches)!

Carol J. Sulcoski is a former attorney turned knitting designer and hand-dyer. She is the author of *Sock Yarn Studio* and *Lace Yarn Studio*. Her designs have been published in *Vogue Knitting*, *Knit Simple*, *St-Denis Magazine*, *KnitScene*, and various other books and magazines. Her work frequently appears in *Vogue Knitting*. She also founded Black Bunny Fibers (blackbunnyfibers.com), an independent dyeing business creating unique handpainted yarns and fibers, and her patterns can be found on Ravelry and Patternfish. She lives outside Philadelphia with her family.

Index